Alexia's Legacy: Lessons for Leadership and Life

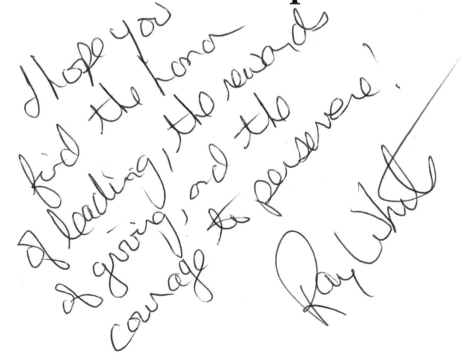

I hope you find the honor of leading, the rewards of giving, and the courage to persevere!

Ray White

Other Books Written by Ray White:

Connecting Happiness and Success – A Guide to Creating Success Through Happiness

Happiness Hacks – Happiness in Under 2 Minutes

Daily Happiness App

Share Smiles, Rate Your Happiness, record and review the things that make you happy, and get Daily Happiness Reminders and Happiness Tips.

You can find tools, resources, Happiness Hacks, and more at ConnectingHappinessandSuccess.com.

Foreword

Alexia Ardeleanu was tragically killed by a drunk driver in 2014, but the leadership lessons she embodied are preserved and shared on the following pages.

This book is about real life lessons in leadership - not just the theories and ideas, but what a leader really does. What are the imperfect actions that result in the leadership we eventually witnessed? We are pulling real life stories, often in Alexia's own words or the words of those she impacted, and using them as examples of what you can do to become a leader and a success. Each story is followed by a summary of what you can learn and an opportunity for you to practice being a leader right now. We hope you find the book impactful and helpful and that Alexia's legacy will be to continue to help others.

100% of the profits of this book will be donated to the Alexia Ardeleanu Memorial Fund.

You can donate to the fund at: **https://one.unt.edu/alexia**

Alexia's Legacy: Lessons for Leadership and Life

Ray White and Austin Hatcher

Xilo Media

Dallas, Texas

Published in the United States by Xilo Media

Library of Congress Control Number: 2014919299

Xilo Media, Lewisville Texas

ISBN 978-0-692-32055-6

Printed in the United States of America

1 3 5 7 9 10 11 8 6 4 2

Edition 1.0

To Connie and Bessie whose courage and perseverance through the worst of times is an inspiration to us all.

To the University of North Texas Professional Leadership Program: Moulding students into future leaders is a noble and worthy cause.

Acknowledgments

Special thanks to Billy Johnson and Rachel Cleveland for helping pull all of the material together and for doing such a great job leading and building the University of North Texas Leadership Program. Thanks to Hunter Blanks and Claire Billingsley for their leadership on the board.

Also thanks to the many people who contributed their heartfelt personal stories. The sincerity, emotion, and appreciation that was shared is impactful and thought provoking. Stories were shared by: Ashley Dixon, Julie Hagen, Marla Ross, Jennifer Ciocan, Kellie Morris, Jamie Graham, Eric Johnson, Isaac Guajardo, Ratinder Sandhu, Karolyn Hernandez, Jena, Christopher Jackson, Sujey Franco, Angelique Davis, Eva Gulin, Nehlin Mehra, Melissa Argueta, Alexis Harrison, Vanessa Arias, Anisha Upponi, Anushka Maya Singh, Regina Torres, Destiny Johnson, Rudy Cerda, Laura Poole, Blake Jackson, Mardon Navalta, Jordyn Williams, and Trey Yates, Jesse Brackeen, Lana and Stephen, Valerie Kite, Kaitlin Nicolson, Teresa and Tony Piraino, Larissa McClain, Lorena Ortiz, Kim Peterson, Jeff Clayton, Kevin Theang, Melony Quinn, Marilyn Wiley, Neal Smatresk.

Thanks to our editors Lindsey White, Rachel Cleveland, Billy Johnson, Wayne Irwin, and Nonie Jobe.

Contents

Contents (continued)

Contents (continued)

Life is not determined by what you are given, but by what you are willing to give.

Ray White

Ray White and Alexia Ardeleanu after a Happiness Speech

Introduction

On June 15th, 2014, Father's Day, the unthinkable happened - that moment in your life that you can never imagine, except in your worst nightmares. Alexia Ardeleanu, a beautiful young lady with unlimited potential was suddenly and tragically taken from us by a drunk driver. The drunk driver who killed her was driving 82 miles an hour when she plowed into Alexia's car and others that were stopped at a stoplight in Houston, Texas.

We spent a lot of time crying and still want to cry every time we think about it. But we have chosen instead to honor her memory. We want to share the lessons she taught us and we feel she would have taught others, if she had been given the time. Alexia was special in what she accomplished and in how she lived her life. She had a perfect 4.0 Grade Point Average in a double major of Accounting and Finance at the University of North Texas. She had taken her GMAT and was working on her LSAT so she could get double graduate degrees in Law and an MBA. She was successful in her job and was a campus leader. She was a Resident Assistant, had won multiple scholarships, and was President of the University of North Texas Professional Leadership Program. But most importantly she was a wonderful friend, daughter, and servant leader. She was special because of her daily focus on the important things in her life and how she unconditionally gave to others.

We want to emphasize that she was not perfect and that was what made her special. The leadership lessons we learned from Alexia are techniques anyone can learn and apply. She was not successful because of natural gifts; she was successful because she made choices every day that led her to be successful and a true servant leader. Our goal in this book is to share her real life examples and choices so you can learn how to make these lessons work for you. We hope that you can see the obstacles and challenges all successful people face and can learn how to persevere and live a life of happiness, success, and servant leadership.

Note from co-author Ray White:

I was lucky enough to be a mentor for Alexia; and as in most of my Mentor/Mentee relationships, I definitely learned as much from her as she did from me. In this book you will see a lot of emails addressed to me from Alexia. Our relationship included daily updates about how she was doing and whether she was on track for reaching the goals in her life and more importantly being happy and successful. We focused a lot on making sure she made taking care of herself a priority and took time for the actions necessary to keep her healthy and happy so she would have the energy be a successful servant leader for others. These emails are a great way to capture what she was thinking and what was really going on in her life. They give us the opportunity to not only see the important characteristics of a good leader but also to observe the concerns, challenges and imperfections as well.

We have structured this book to show real life examples from Alexia or people she interacted with, a summary of the lesson, and then an opportunity to help you reflect and improve on your related leadership skills.

We hope you enjoy the book and learn the reality about how you can be a servant leader who is both successful and happy.

Create Leadership Habits

Lesson #1 - Create Leadership Habits Before You Become the Leader

My very first brush with Alexia by Austin Hatcher

I first met Alexia when I started the Professional Leadership Program (PLP) at UNT. Alexia and I both shared the desire to sit as front and center as we could during the Wednesday meetings. For the majority of my time in PLP that was all I knew about her. It was not until PLP was almost over that I really got a glimpse of her character.

PLP was winding down for the end of the school year and the PLP Directors had asked for those interested in holding a student director position to apply and prepare for an interview. A student director for PLP is responsible for planning, structuring and executing a fair amount of the program. So in short student directors carry some real weight in affecting people's lives for better or worse.

I am one of the most competitive people I know and have always had a ridiculous drive to be better. While I am competitive I have learned to never underestimate your competition. I applied for the President, Vice President and Marketing Student Director positions for the 2013-14 year. Needless to say I was swinging for the top. So when interview day came around, I felt I did well, and maybe even knocked it out of the park. I even had two goals and several ideas for improvement so I felt I had an edge up on the competition. I found out that I made Vice President and my competitive side was thinking, "Where was I inadequate?" I finally started talking to Alexia about her ideas and realized she pretty much wrote a book on her plans for

PLP. She had a thorough structured plan on exactly what she would do as president to make PLP better for the students. This was only the beginning of my realization that she truly had that "something special".

If you had compared Alexia's interview notes and mine you would have likely found a few differences and what made her special. It was like looking at a random rock vs. a work of art that had been created with hours of work. I had a few "Big Picture" goals scribbled on some paper and was ready to explain them further if needed, but Alexia had detailed notes. She had plans to make sure that every minute of PLP's time was productive. What made her more special is that Alexia understood that productive doesn't always mean work out the door. She knew she was dealing with people and that people have other needs. Alexia had a detailed agenda of her changes and was ready to execute. She was just so amazingly prepared. Her plan was organized and focused. She wanted to be a lawyer and would have no doubt been one of the best.

The other thing that made her special was that she was the hardest and smartest worker I've ever met. Besides working towards becoming valedictorian, she was involved in campus organizations, was a Resident Assistant in the Honors Hall, was an active participant in the PLP, and still had time for fun. Everything Alexia did was done with excellence because it came from her heart. She was always prepared and she took preparation seriously because she understood that when you are prepared everything is better for everyone. She knew that good planning set up a positive chain reaction of events. Alexia was constantly looking for blind spots and ways to improve; she then structured a way to execute her plans and make it easy for others to comprehend.

She never forgot that she was dealing with humans either. What I found out as I got to see her in action - what truly made her one of a kind - is that she worked hard for others and not just her own gain. After we talked about her notes at school we decided to meet in the middle of summer for additional planning, because we didn't want the people we were "responsible" for not to get our best. We met at Johnny Carino's in Lewisville, Texas because she loved that place. That was when I got to see her plans first-hand.

She wanted to get on the same page with me and make sure we could communicate and be aligned in our PLP goals.

The other thing that she did well was take feedback. She wasn't emotionally attached to her ideas, but rather cared about the best results. We went through each other's goals with complete humility. It is hard to find talented and humble 4.0 GPA superstars. She was a big picture thinker who had people as the basis of her motivation. That was Alexia, always planning to plan, but only because she cared about others!

Lesson: Create leadership habits before you become the leader.

Alexia didn't become a leader when she was elected president of the Professional Leadership Program. Years before she began developing habits that made her a good leader. She was organized, focused, and most importantly, she cared about the people she wanted to lead. She didn't approach the role claiming she deserved to be leader. She brought her skills and habits to the table with humility and passion. She had a plan and a vision and she showed the team what she could help them accomplish. She asked for input and listened to ideas. She motivated Austin and other team members to start planning and preparing early. She worked hard daily and weekly so that when the leadership opportunity arrived, it wasn't a big deal for her to step into the role, it was a natural transition.

In later chapters we will teach you how to create positive habits of organization, goal setting, discipline, nurturing relationships, gratitude, and taking care of yourself one day at a time. Then, when the time comes to lead, you can seamlessly step into the role and contribute to the success and happiness of the team.

Opportunity: Pick a leadership trait (see lessons in following chapters) you can nurture until it becomes a habit, e.g. Organization Skills, Goal Setting, Discipline, Nurturing Relationships, Practicing Gratitude, or Taking Care of Yourself.

Lesson #2 - Practice Gratitude

Alexia and Gratitude by Austin Hatcher

Alexia was not just a worker and all business. She liked to have fun too and loved to make others feel appreciated. She often spent her own money so that the student directors would know she appreciated us. She would tell us thank you, bring food to the meetings, bring birthday cakes and sneak thank you cards into our folders. Alexia also made sure our personal lives were going well. She wanted us (and others) to always know we were valued and that she appreciated us - not just business thanks, but personal as well. Stopping in the midst of your busy day to simply say thank you verbally and with your actions is paramount for good leadership. Every person wants to feel they are an appreciated part of something bigger and Alexia was great at making that happen. Warmth and respect were the feelings you would get when you were in her presence.

A few examples from Alexia's emails:

"Thank you so much and I will see you in the morning!"

"Tonight I wrote a bunch of thank you cards for all the leaders and execs at McKesson that helped make the internship so memorable for me... It made me feel very grateful for everything they have done for me. After writing all 15 or so of them, it really put into perspective for me just how lucky I have been to meet with, speak with, and/or work with all of them! It was definitely rewarding!"

"I will say it's getting harder to find things to be grateful for just because the bigger, more obvious ones I always say I don't want to reuse. Because of that, it is keeping me humbled and thinking about all the smaller things as well that people, as well as I, tend to take for granted."

"For journals, I am writing about things I am grateful for, accomplishments, and dreams. Dreams and things I am grateful for are getting a bit harder trying not to reuse anything but it makes me think a little harder and think on the littler things which is good."

Karolyn,

Great update for everyone! Thank you so much for this! Melissa has completed the hours and was having lunch with the director who can verify that last Friday so she should just need to turn in the form. I will double check though!

Alexia

Lesson: Practice gratitude.

Gratitude helps you be happier and helps your team feel good about their contributions. We often take for granted the things and people around us and just expect that we will always have cars to drive, a place to live, and a good job. But many people have much less. Because we think people are supposed to deliver on their commitments, we forget to thank them and appreciate the work they put in. Take time to be grateful for the hundreds of things you have. Our reality is created in part by what we choose to see and focus on. By looking for things to be grateful for, your focus and therefore your reality is filled with what is good in your life instead of what is not. Take time to show gratitude for everything your team delivers. You will be happier, you will have better relationships, and you will be a better leader.

Opportunity: Think of three things you are grateful for every morning.

Lesson #3 - Share Your Smile

Alexia was among the most beautiful people I knew on campus. Her beauty was not merely external: it was also internal. This inner beauty shined through her speech, her actions, her attitude, her schedule, her bearing, and her smile. I remember a number of times coming down to the front desk of Honors Hall with questions and concerns, and Alexia was so helpful and kind. She was a hard and determined worker. I was amazed after hearing about everything she was involved in. Her drive was motivating and inspiring. Amidst school and work, Alexia still had time for Honors Hall, her residents, and her friends. Even when she was faced with stress, she dealt with it in a composed manner.

Every time I walked into Honors Hall, and Alexia was in the lobby or working the front desk, she always made it a point to smile or say, "Hi, Julie! How are you?" Even though she probably never realized it, those hellos really meant a lot to me.

At the conclusion of this spring's semester, a huge number of exciting doors opened in my life. When Alexia heard about them, she gave me a huge hug and a joyful "Congratulations!" I came to Alexia with some problems and I knew that if I ever needed help with something personal and troubling, I could go to her. I felt so comfortable around her. She made herself approachable and available to any who needed her.

The thing that will always stand out in my mind when I think of Alexia Ardeleanu is her smile. Her smile was contagious, so joyful, and happy. It was a very rare occasion to see her without it.

Julie Hagen, Honors Hall Resident

My most prominent memory of Alexia is her uplifting attitude. Even when I saw her very busy with a lot of things on her plate, I don't recall ever seeing her with a negative attitude. She made such an effort to make me feel welcome on staff that I looked forward to running in to her.   Marla Ross

Alexia always knew how to cheer me up with her genuine, sweet smile and words of encouragement that honestly lifted my spirit more than most people could.   Jennifer Ciocan

Our first Starbuck's stop, in Forney, Tx on our Florida road trip, May 2014. When I (Suzanne Peterson, on the left) got an internship in Florida, Alexia (on the right) dropped everything and offered to drive down with me. Alexia would do anything for her friends. Actually, not just her friends - Alexia would do anything for any of the people in her life. She was the quintessential servant leader. Our first semester of school, Alexia overheard a friend of a friend talking about how she was unsure of how she'd get home to Houston. Alexia and I had a trip planned for the next weekend and she offered this girl a ride, I was shocked that Alexia would do that for someone who was almost a stranger. It turned out that I was right and that trip home turned out to be the worst road trip of our lives. But we retold that "traumatic" story and laughed about it for years. Even when it made things worse for herself, Alexia always went out of her way to make things better for others. From our first road trip in Fall 2011 when we met to our last one to Florida, I saw her do this hundreds of times. Suzanne Peterson

Lesson: Share your smile.

Your smile is one of the best gifts you can share with the world. It is easy and doesn't cost anything. It communicates warmth, welcome, and caring. Your smile is viral and will make others want to smile. Smiling actually releases a chemical in your brain that makes you happier. People who see your smile will instinctually mimic it and it will make them happier. It will then spread to other people who see them smiling. Practice smiling. Share your smile with everyone. It makes more difference than you could ever imagine.

Opportunity: Think about whether you are so focused on team and personal challenges that you are walking around with a grimace on your face, or are you taking a few moments to appreciate life and share your smile with others?

Alexia with square donuts our very first time at Denton Square Donuts in Fall 2011. This was one of first study sessions. Alexia always kept me productive. To get me up early though she had to bribe me with donuts. Suzanne

Lesson #4 - Leadership is <u>Not</u> All Roses and

Sunshine

Ray,

It was not exactly drama. More like feedback and critique from some of the SDs (Student Directors) concerning them getting involved in the program and their role as SD's and how we recruit members. It was a very long conversation which seemed more like venting for a few SDs. I will fill you in fully on Monday.

Alexia

Ray,

After I went to the accounting lab to work on my project, I found my error! It was purely an adding error, not a conceptual error, so no wonder I was so lost as to where I went wrong! I have almost all of my statements created after working on it a lot today, so I am feeling pretty good about where I am at with it!

I also am happy that we didn't have points of concern in our staff meeting today. Everything happens for a reason and I am really thinking that the reason it was skipped in staff tonight was to give me time to help the others see the situation in the way that you helped me today. After speaking with you, I definitely am feeling a lot better about it all. When little things started to come up today, it was easy for me to take a deep breath and not let it affect my mood or ruin my productivity... Now I just need to focus on keeping that perspective when time passes and more little things keep piling up again!

Thanks again for being such an amazing mentor, helping me keep the focus on what's best for me first so that I can be in a better state when I help others, and just helping me keep a positive perspective when things get a bit crazy! I am very thankful for having you as my mentor!

Have a great night and thank you again for everything!

Alexia

Ray,

This morning I took it a bit slow and slept in more than normal to help kick the recurring fever I have been having on and off all weekend... I think it helped, because today is the first day in four days without a fever all day!

That helped me be pretty productive this evening in preparation for my classes.

In addition, today we (PLP SDs) had another pretty productive meeting. I have been sending out some basic info and a list of things that we all need to have prepared before the meeting the day before and that has seemed to really help! <u>We now need to get a budget put together for our end of year event and its coming easier to some then others.... That's our next big challenge!</u>

I'm now off to do my journals and head to bed!

Alexia

Lesson: Leadership is not all roses and sunshine.

As you progress as a leader you will go from a few followers to most of the group following. At that point, the other leaders in the group will start pushing you to be better. It will often manifest itself as criticism and complaining, but it is a very important step in your growth as a leader. It is your opportunity to cull the positive lessons from all the noise, and to show your team that you hear them and will act on their behalf. This action can solidify your position as a leader and give you confidence to take on the bigger challenges.

Opportunity: Think about and journal what the tough situations are teaching you?

Lesson #5 - Turn Bad Days into Good Days

Ray,

Today has been an interesting day. I worked the desk a lot to fill in for our full time clerk that is gone, was given the run around on multiple things I was trying to get done, and got a massage because my neck, shoulders, and back were starting to get sore again.

However, upside of the day, I went to dinner with Tiffany and Alison (some McKesson people) after they were done working the UNT career fair. We had a really great talk both personally and professionally! We talked a lot about ways to improve the internship program, which Alison is in charge of, and a lot about opportunities for me to stay with McKesson after undergrad and while going to law school. It was a great end to a rather dull and routine day!

I'm now off to bed to get some rest while I can!

Alexia

Lesson: Turn bad days into good days.

Every day good things and bad things happen to us. We can choose to focus on the bad and whine and complain or we can choose to focus on the good and remember the joyful moments. In a month we will not remember the details of each day. We will only remember the highlights and how we ended the day feeling. If we end the day reviewing everything that went wrong, a month from now, we will remember a bad day. If we end the day reviewing what was great with our world, then a month from now we will remember today as a good day. Spend a week ending your day with good thoughts and you will remember a good week. Spend a month, and you will remember good months. Spend a year and you will be on your way to living a lifetime of great years.

Opportunity: Consider what went well today?

Fun in the "snow" Spring 2012. Alexia and I were both from the Houston area; and therefore didn't get very many snowy days. The snow here barely stuck to the ground and melted very quickly, but we had so much fun and stayed out there for hours scraping it off the ground and throwing the mush at each other.   Suzanne Peterson

Lesson #6 - Life Can Be Overwhelming

Ray,

I'm not sure if you got my email this past week or not (now that my work email isn't active, my phone was out of sync with my different email accounts - I am pretty sure I fixed it now though!).

However, to fill you in, I finally have all of my stuff put away and organized at the apartment! It's a great feeling! My parents are probably coming up this weekend to bring me a few more things from home and to see me because I have not been home in almost two months and won't be able to make it home for at least another two and a half weeks!

Work has had some added pressure due to the fact our department needs to get a project prepped for the new intern who starts in a week! There's a lot we all need to do and it's definitely keeping me busy!

On top of all of that, the LSAT is in two weeks! I'm prepping in hopes that I will be ready to take it. However, I still feel like I need A LOT more repetition with the material. My LSAT professor says we will have the "are you ready for the June exam" talk next week, so I am hoping for a lot of light bulbs to go off between now and then!

I hope you are doing well and I am sorry things have been so crazy that I haven't kept as in touch as I should have these past few weeks!

Talk to you soon!

Alexia

Ray,

Sorry for no email yesterday. I laid down in bed and passed out before I picked up my phone to send it!

Yesterday PLP went VERY well. We had a very efficient SD meeting which resulted in a very smooth member meeting as well! I would argue that it was one of our best Wednesdays yet!

Today was full of classes and meetings. By the end of the day <u>I felt like my brain was on overload working out when I am going to do what and how to get it all done.... Then some friends invited me to go see a movie and I thought that might be just the thing to settle my mind!</u> I just got home and am headed to bed!

Talk to you soon,

Alexia

Lesson: Life can be overwhelming.

The list of things you have to do at any point in time can be overwhelming. Each day more and more keeps coming at you. You have things you know you should be doing, but you just can't seem to get to them. We live in a 24/7 always on world. With instant access to information and communication on our phones and other devices, we have a never ending stream of demands and distractions.

In the midst of all this chaos, it is important to stop and recognize how overwhelming life can be. Pause and recognize that we really can't do it all. Once we are clear that life is overwhelming and that we can't do it all, then we can start prioritizing and focusing on what we can do.

Life is not about getting as much done as we can. Life is about getting the most important things done. Even as a leader, your goal is not to do it all. Happiness and success do not come from doing it all. Happiness and success come from doing what is important. Focus on the things where you can matter and make a difference in someone's life. Do one thing at a time and then move on to the next. When you feel overwhelmed, as we all do, stop and pick one thing that is important and get that done. Everything else can wait and/or be rescheduled. Once your first priority is completed, move on to the next. This will seem difficult at first, but you will feel more fulfilled and content tackling one important task at a time, rather than being overwhelmed by the never-ending train of things to do.

Opportunity: Stop, breathe, and focus on what's important. A movie or dinner with your friends, or time with your family is just as important as studying for the LSAT or getting an A. Make time for both. Take time to enjoy the path you are on.

Lesson #7 - Take Time to Appreciate When Things

Go Right

Ray,

I will definitely take a look at this over the break and let you know what I think!

This week has been amazing so far! Nothing has been too stressful, nothing has been too pressing, everyone has been incredibly nice, and I have been getting to sleep earlier than normal!

We had a PLP SD holiday dinner tonight so I didn't get home until after ten but I have gotten all settled in and am already curled up in bed ready to fall asleep!

Talk to you soon!

Alexia

From Alexia's Journal:

I am thankful for:
- *The McKinsey Consulting Meeting*
- *Time to call my parents*
- *Such beautiful weather*

Lesson: Take time to appreciate when things go right.

Celebrate your small successes. Take a few moments to stop and appreciate the things that are going right. As leaders, we are often caught up in all the challenges and problems we need to solve. We have long to-do lists that seem like they will never be completed. So as a leader, you have to consciously stop and appreciate what is going right and what you have accomplished. Celebrate small successes, personally, and with your team.

Opportunity: Every day, email a friend with a list of things that went right for you personally and for your team.

Lesson #8 - Appreciate Progress

Ray,

Not too much different to report today. I did take the verbal section of the GMAT practice exam and feel decent with where I placed given it is the first practice exam. I placed in the 81st percentile. I still want better, but not a bad start!

Alexia

Ray,

Today has been a SUPER productive day, personally, professionally, and academically! I have very few things left on my "to do" list! I just finished packing for tomorrow and am now off to complete my journals and head to bed! Talk to you soon!

Alexia

From Alexia's Journal:

Today I accomplished:
- *Part 2 of Policy Boards*
- *Finished Resident Door Decks*
- *Room Inventories*

Lesson: Appreciate progress.

Take a moment to appreciate what you have accomplished and build from there rather than being completely disappointed and giving up because of what you have not accomplished. Celebrate the small successes daily, rather than waiting for the big successes that come once a year or once a decade. Build your confidence by recognizing the small accomplishments and the good days. Leaders should keep the long term goal in mind, but they also have to appreciate the small steps and progress that are occurring daily to keep the team motivated and moving forward. Leaders help the team focus on the next step rather than getting discouraged by how high up the mountain they eventually have to climb. Appreciate and reward daily progress.

Opportunity: Share with your team the small steps they team accomplished today?

Lesson #9 – Lead By Example

My name is Nick Grotowski, and I was one of the RAs at Honors Hall with Alexia. It's difficult to even fathom the idea of putting into words Alexia's impact on my life. Since I started my time at Honors Hall, Alexia treated me like family. She was always willing to go completely out of her way just to do me one small favor. I often remember trying to switch an on-call or desk shift, and it seemed like she was willing to change an entire week's worth of her schedule just so I could have some convenience. This is only one example of how she was completely selfless. Throughout the entire year, I felt her unconditional love and caring, and for that I'm eternally grateful.

I also want to mention the impact that Alexia will continue to have on me for the rest of my life. Knowing her provided me with a gifted role model that I will continue to look to for guidance. I've discussed with a few close friends how Alexia was always associated with a bright future. If she ever came up in conversation, without fail, we ended up talking about her drive and dedication. And as I face typical difficulties in everyday life – a huge pile of homework, a lack of sleep – I often think back to Alexia and her determination to achieve, and those thoughts are always inspiring. Nick Grotowski

I only knew her for a year, but Alexia left such a lasting impact on me in that year. Her determination and professionalism were a huge inspiration to me. Anytime I thought a task would get the better of me, I would think of Alexia and how, with all the things she had going on, she always managed to get everything done on time. I can only hope that one day I will be half the ambitious professional she was.   Kellie Morris

She was such a good friend and always a great motivator for those around her. She always had a high standard for herself and surpassed it with her unmatched drive.   *Jamie Graham*

Alexia spent each day working hard to reach her goals through persistence, self-discipline and enlightenment. She took every opportunity to lift her friends' spirits. My favorite memories with her were when we got up early in the mornings to go to Starbucks each week during one semester to study for our Real Estate Law class. I would take the notes over the even chapters and she had the odd chapters; then we would supply the other with our notes so that we covered every chapter. I had to always stay up late the night before we were going to study because I'd wait until the last minute to type up my three chapters worth of notes for the next morning. I didn't ever have to ask if she would have her's done; I was such a terrible procrastinator for that class, so to keep from making her mad at me, I'd triple up on monsters and Redbull and try to get it all done by the time she picked me up at 7am. Many times I'd not even sleep. She'd ask if everything was okay because I looked terrible and never once did I tell her I practically went through hell the night before to make sure she had her notes. I never told her because she had high expectations of me; just like she had of everyone else she was friends with. If Alexia had high expectations of you, it meant she saw the potential in you to succeed and accomplish whatever you meant to accomplish and she was willing to help you get there. For someone of her character and prestige to see that in a person is very special. She taught me by example, what it looks like to work toward your dreams daily in a very realistic way; and just recently that it's not about how much time we have but what we do with the time we have left.   *Ashley Dixon*

Lesson: Lead by example.

A lot of leadership occurs without you even realizing it. Are you modeling behaviors that others would like to emulate? Do you reach out to people and make yourself available? What kind of behavior are others observing? A significant amount of leadership is in your own self-discipline and the choices you make. Whether you want to be a leader or not, people are observing your actions and deciding whether they want to emulate your behavior or avoid it. Focus on your priorities and caring about others. The more self-discipline and success you show, and the more caring and helpful you are, the more willing they will be to follow you. Everyone struggles with doing what is right vs. what is easy. Set the example for them and show them it can be done. Show them that besides accomplishing more they can be happier and more fulfilled. Care enough about them to lead them to something better. You are an example whether you know it or not and whether you want to be or not. So be a good example. It will make you better and it will help you help others believe and grow. Be the best you can be and others will follow.

On a side note, this does not mean trying to be perfect. People would actually prefer to follow a leader who is imperfect and more like them. Be yourself, but be your "best" self. Don't worry that people might be watching; focus on doing the right thing for you and the team.

Opportunity: Determine how you can be a better example today?

Eating goldfish while crossing the Florida state line May 2014. Alexia asked me what I wanted for car snacks, and I said goldfish. Alexia, knowing full well that she wasn't going to help eat the goldfish, bought me the biggest carton that exists. My five roommates and I are still working on this box of goldfish.   Suzanne Peterson

Lesson #10 - Make an Impact

I had the privilege and luck to know and work with Alexia for a year and a half. In that time I found she was kind hearted, professional, and a joy to work with and know as a friend. As a Resident Assistant for about a year before Alexia arrived at Honors Hall I thought I had a measure for the kind of people I would encounter at my job. Alexia surpassed my expectations. It isn't hyperbole to state that by the end of her first week she knew more about being a good RA than I did. Outside of work she brought a fire to the honors hall community that never existed before her.   *Eric Johnson*

Lesson: Make an impact.

How do you move through the world? You can demand the world adapt and change to your needs or you can make a positive impact and leave good feelings wherever you go. You can "go through the motions" and exert as little effort as possible or you can bring your passion and creativity to your job and other leadership opportunities. As a leader, make it your goal to impact people's lives in a positive manner. Take passion and caring into every project and every job. Try to make a difference.

Opportunity: Find out where can you make an impact today?

Integrate Goals into Your Life

Lesson #11 - Put Your Goals in Writing

From Alexia's Journal: *I want to go to a great law school & become a corporate lawyer.*

Alexia's Goals August 2013

Professional Learning and Development Goals
Goal 1: Make a decision about whether to go CPA/JD or JD/MBA
Goal 2: Evaluate my relationship with McKesson to be able to decide their role in the rest of my college career.
Goal 3: Gain a better working knowledge of LinkedIn

Personal Goals
Goal 1: Improve work life balance techniques
Goal 2: Maintain 4.0 GPA
Goal 3: Create a working budget

[Note: Alexia's goals also included plans and due dates not shown here]

PLP Goals Alexia Helped Set as Leader

Professional Leadership Program
Goal 1: Develop stakeholders; students, mentors, and faculty
Goal 2: Create a family-like culture
Goal 3: Create communication that supports connections and relationships, and exemplifies our brand

Lesson: Put your goals in writing.

"First, have a definite, clear, practical ideal; a goal, an objective."　Aristotle

Goals are an important part of leadership, both for setting an example and for helping the team move forward. Setting goals helps us align today's actions with the future. What do you want to accomplish and what are you doing today that will help you get there? People without goals meander through life experiencing random events that don't lead them down any discernible path. They engage in activity without progress. Goals focus our actions to a self-chosen path and bring pattern and clarity to what would otherwise be a haphazard menagerie of experiences.

Make your goals specific and challenging, yet achievable. Have a set date for accomplishment, and make them measurable so you can objectively evaluate your progress.

Writing down your goals is the first step to achieving them. Written goals can be more easily shared with your friends which significantly improves your chances of achieving those goals. Most importantly, written goals give you something to refer back to that refreshes your memory. As our lives get busy, the goals get pushed to the background; and we need to re-read them to bring them back to being part of our conscious intentions. Once our goals are in writing we can objectively evaluate our progress in reaching those goals on a regular basis.

Opportunity: Write 3 goals you want accomplish this year.

My Goals
Goal 1:
Goal 2:
Goal 3:

Alexia's 21st birthday at a wolf sanctuary in Montgomery, TX

Lesson #12 - Every Goal Needs an Action Plan

Alexia's Goals August 2013 with Action Plans

Professional Learning and Development Goals	Action Plan
Goal 1: Make a decision about whether to go CPA/JD or JD/MBA	1. Meet with counselor to discuss academic feasibility. 2. Meet with 7 professionals to gain input and perspective 3. Speak with top 3 law schools to see if credits will transfer from MA to MBA or JD
Goal 2: Evaluate my relationship with McKesson to be able to decide their role in the rest of my college career.	1. Can I work and maintain my 4.0 GPA 2. Do they have a place for me in the spring? 3. Can I make enough money to meet my budget goals
Goal 3: Gain a better working knowledge of LinkedIn	1. Meet with Rachel 2. Study Linked-in Presentations 3. Build my profile

Personal Goals	Action Plan
Goal 1: Improve work life balance techniques	1. Create Scheduled "Me" time. 1 hour – 3 times per week 2. Exercise. 30 minutes – 4 times per week
Goal 2: Maintain 4.0 GPA	1. Study at minimum 3 hours per day
Goal 3: Create a working budget	1. Meet with Student Money Management Center

PLP Goals Alexia Helped Set as Leader

Professional Leadership Program	Action Plan
Goal 1: Develop stakeholders; students, mentors, and faculty	1. Improve class offerings 2. Member/Mentor Review program 3. Recruit new majors to PLP 4. Increase involvement of Faculty
Goal 2: Create a family-like culture	1. Create engagement opportunities outside of normal meetings 2. Focus on clusters 3. Increase mentor involvement
Goal 3: Create communication that supports connections and relationships, and exemplifies our brand	1. Thank you letter process 2. Post events on social media 3. Encourage stakeholder involvement in media sites 4. Create Student Director bonding time

Lesson: Every goal needs an action plan.

Once we set our goals, we need to build and implement an action plan that will get us there. Most importantly, we always need to know our next step. Notice that several of Alexia's goals were related to making decisions. Her plans related to how she would collect the info she needed to make those decisions. The plans also had multiple steps so there was a clear path to accomplishment. Create a plan for each of your goals. Clarify the steps in your plan, even if those steps include brainstorming next steps. One of the keys to goal accomplishment is understanding that it is more important to visualize the steps it will take to get there than to visualize accomplishment of the goal itself. Focus on your action plan and always keep your next step top of mind.

Opportunity: Create Action Plans for Your Goals

Lesson #13 - Every Goal Needs a Due Date

Alexia's Goals August 2013 with Due Dates

Professional Learning and Development Goals	Due Date
Goal 1: Make a decision about whether to go CPA/JD or JD/MBA	September 30, 2013
Goal 2: Evaluate my relationship with McKesson to be able to decide their role in the rest of my college career.	October 31, 2013
Goal 3: Gain a better working knowledge of LinkedIn	December 31, 2013

Personal Goals	Due Date
Goal 1: Improve work life balance techniques	Every week
Goal 2: Maintain 4.0 GPA	December 2013
Goal 3: Create a working budget	March 2014

Lesson: Every goal needs a due date.

Another key to goal accomplishment is setting due dates for your goals. In order to objectively measure goal accomplishment, you need to know when it will be accomplished. Set reachable dates that challenge you but you feel comfortable you can achieve. Often when you first set a goal you don't have all the information to know exactly when it can be accomplished. If you find out new information and need to change your due dates, don't hesitate to make the change. The worse thing you can do is get focused on a due date you don't believe you can hit. Don't stress if you miss a due date. Create a new due date and keep moving forward.

Due dates help you, as a leader, hold your team accountable. They provide a sense of urgency and serve as a catalyst for the team to take action now rather than delaying next steps indefinitely.

Opportunity: Set due dates for each of your goals.

Lesson #14 - Memorize Your Goals

Ray,

I hope you had a safe flight! This weekend I have gotten a lot done for PLP, classes, and RA. I have had to make a great effort to be sure and take some mental breaks so I didn't/ don't burn out! I was also able to take some "me time", some exercising time, and some time to <u>glance over my goals to help keep them in the forefront of my mind</u>. I got a lot done but I still have A LOT to do tomorrow, so I am off to bed to try and get some sleep!

Talk to you soon,

Alexia

Lesson: Memorize your goals.

Writing down your goals is not enough. You need to review them every day until they become a constant part of your thought process. Very few people write down their goals, but even fewer take the time to memorize them and think about them daily. Being a good leader requires you and your team to be vigilant about understanding and constantly working toward your goals. Write your goals down and spend two minutes every day reading them until you can recite them word for word from memory.

Opportunity: Read your goals over and over until they are memorized.

Lesson #15 - Include Taking Care of Yourself in Your Personal Goals

Alexia had to set goals about taking care of herself. It didn't just happen. She was too busy. She had to make a conscious effort.

Personal Goals	Action Plan
Goal 1: Improve work life balance techniques	1. Create Scheduled "Me" time. 1 hour – 3 times per week 2. Exercise. 30 minutes – 4 times per week
Goal 2: Maintain 4.0 GPA	1. Study at minimum 3 hours per day
Goal 3: Create a working budget	1. Meet with Student Money Management Center

Ray,

"My me time this week went well. I had some quiet time each night as well as some time with friends. That was not a challenge with this week's schedule. As for exercising, it wasn't the typical week either. I spent one night at my friends' house for an hour swimming laps with her and then went to the gym another night for an hour. So I met the total time for the week but not the number of days... I need to work on that a bit more this coming week"

Alexia

Ray,

"*After work today, I moved a lot of my stuff back up to Denton and got it situated there so I have been staying a bit active all evening. I'm just getting home and am about to do 15 minutes of exercise, write in my journals and head to bed! Hopefully that will help me get a good night sleep and I will be able to get up nice and early and feel a bit more rested and refreshed!* "

Alexia

Ray,

So a few things I did today was my me time, my exercise time, got all of the agenda and power point presentations for PLP tomorrow put together, and finished filling in the scorecard (there are a few things I want to check with Rachel about tomorrow and then I will send it your way!). It has been a very productive day! I am now writing my journals and am off to bed!

Alexia

Ray,

Today has been a long day! I went into work this morning, ran some errands and got home around seven. I then fell asleep around eight. I didn't realize how tired I really was! I'm doing my journals and am headed to bed for the night now! Hopefully I will be able to wake up early, get a good work out in and start a productive day!

Alexia

Lesson: Include taking care of yourself in your personal goals.

As a leader, you will find yourself often overbooked and overwhelmed. Your responsibilities to your team, helping others, and your other commitments in life will suck away all of your free time. Often the first thing to fall off your schedule is time for your sleep, exercise, and downtime. You can't be a good leader if are sick in bed or burned out. Bad health and too much stress can complicate your life and lead to bad decisions, short attention spans, and a lack of the patience that the people on your team deserve. Also, as a leader you want to set a good example and show your team that taking care of yourself is a priority. When they see you making the right decisions, they will feel they have permission to also make the right decisions. Make taking care of yourself and your health a top priority. Make time for friends and family, make time to exercise and eat right, and be sure you get enough sleep.

Opportunity: Set three goals related to taking care of yourself.

Lesson #16 - Don't Just Set Your Goals, Revisit Them Again and Again, and Revise as Needed

October 2013

Ray,

Today has been a busy day! I feel pretty confident that I got an A on my exam today! We hopefully will find out on Thursday!

I also reviewed all my goals today and seem to be on track! All the goals due by September are complete and some due October are already in progress-some are actually completed already!

Now I need to be very productive the rest of the week so I'm hoping for a long and peaceful night of rest! Talk to you tomorrow!

Alexia

December 2013

Ray,

Hope you had a great weekend!

This Wednesday our winter scorecards are due. I have gone through and filled out the status of the PLP Scorecard Goals and the goals we set up when we first started meeting in the summer.

I will bring hard copies to our meeting in the morning so we can review them, but I thought you might like to have soft copies as well! See you in the morning!

Alexia

Alexia's Goal Review – December 2013

Professional Learning and Development Goals	Status
Goal 1: Make a decision about whether to go CPA/JD or JD/MBA	Complete – Go with JD/MBA
Goal 2: Evaluate my relationship with McKesson to be able to decide their role in the rest of my college career.	Complete – Great opportunities
Goal 3: Gain a better working knowledge of LinkedIn	Complete

Personal Goals	Status
Goal 1: Improve work life balance techniques	Needs work
Goal 2: Maintain 4.0 GPA	On track
Goal 3: Create a working budget	Complete

[Note: Alexia's goals also included plans and due dates not shown here]

January 2014

Ray,

Today I was able to revisit and adjust my goals for this semester, prepare some things for PLP this week, and worked on some McKesson files for work tomorrow. I just finished reading another chapter of your book and am now about to write in my journals and head to bed! See you in the morning!

Alexia

Alexia's goals after revision in January 2014

Professional Learning and Development Goals	Plan
New Goal 1: Be fully prepared for the GMAT. Shoot for score: 710 (University of Chicago's median is 720 - ranked #1 B-School by Business Weekly)	1. Listen to all ten tutorial lessons online 2. Complete all practice homework problems 3. Review lessons that showed inferior performance on the practice homework problems 4. Take a practice GMAT 5. Review as needed until the exam
New Goal 2: Be fully prepared for the LSAT. Shoot for score: 170 (University of Chicago's median is 171 - ranked #5 for Law Schools)	Complete the LSAT prep class and utilize all materials provided.

Personal Goals	Plan
Goal 1: Improve work life balance techniques	Create Scheduled "Me" time. 1 hour – 3 times per week Exercise. 30 minutes – 4 times per week
Goal 2: Maintain 4.0 GPA	Study at minimum 3 hours per day

March 2014

Ray,

This morning was booked with the last of the RA training sessions. When I got home after lunch, I clocked some hours catching up on McKesson work. I then had dinner with Austin and Chaney and went over some things in preparation for tomorrow, Saturday, and the semester as a whole! When I got home for the evening, I began to revisit and reassess where I stand in regard to my personal goals. I still have a few things to tweak and/or add. As soon as I get that finalized, I will send it your way.

I have had some me time this evening and am now off to complete my journals and head to bed! Talk to you soon

Alexia

Lesson: Don't just set your goals; revisit them again and again, and revise as needed.

One of the key aspects of successful goal-setting is feedback and evaluation on your progress. Written goals provide an objective system for measuring progress. Periodically revisit and re-assess your goals and make adjustments.

Are you successfully reaching your goals and do they need to change? Schedule a day and time each week, or at a minimum, each month, when you will check in on the status of your goals. Objectively evaluate whether you are on track and determine what changes you need to make in your actions and planning for those goals that are not on track.

Also, take to time re-evaluate whether you have the right goals and whether or not they should be changed or adjusted. Are they overwhelming and unrealistic and do you find them more of a burden than a motivator? Do they still align with your plans for the future? If you have already accomplished several of them, do you need to set more goals?

Make adjustments to your goals. Make sure they align with your life and what you want to accomplish. These are your goals, make sure they represent what you want to accomplish rather than what someone else wants you to accomplish. Make sure to re-assess and adjust your goals on a regular basis so they become an integral part of your life rather than a burden or obligation.

Opportunity: Set a scheduled date and time for your next goal review.

Date: _____   **Time:** _____

This is the second time Alexia and I ever hung out. It was Fall 2011, just before classes started. We're walking to Taco Cabana, near Honors Hall, with fellow fourth floor resident James Nichols. This was the first of many of our midnight trips for food. They usually took us to Kerr for tater tots and ice cream. And then we'd come back and sit cross legged on the floor in the hallways and just talk for hours about our lives. Those are some of my favorite memories from freshman year. Suzanne

Lesson #17 - Be Honest with Yourself

Alexia's Personal Evaluation (part of PLP goal setting process)

Accomplishments: Dean's List; McKesson Internship; OSMP Award for RA Job, President of PLP, 4.0 GPA	
Disappointments: Unbalanced work life balance; struggle or stress of sometimes taking on too much/not knowing **healthy** limits	Potential Derailers: Unplanned failures/disappointment; becoming so stressed that I hit the point of being burned out

Lesson: Be honest with yourself.

From the outside, Alexia had a 4.0 with a double major in accounting and finance, was president of the Professional Leadership Program, was doing great at her job, had lots of friends, and seemed to get everything done. But when you look at her disappointments, you see she was just like everyone else with concerns about work/life balance, knowing healthy limits, stress, burnout, and becoming overwhelmed. But Alexia persevered. She recognized these challenges and worked on them daily. Alexia set goals related to taking care of herself and managing the many things on her plate. She did what we all can do, which is be honest with ourselves, admit our challenges, face them head on and work to solve them.

We often work under the mistaken assumption that for successful people everything is easy. They make it look easy so we are not aware of the trials and tribulations they go through to get things done. For Alexia, finding enough time to study was a struggle. But she didn't give up and ignore the goal. She admitted it was a struggle, faced the problem, and believed in herself and her ability to persevere and figure it out. Success does not happen just because everything is going right. Success is a result of persevering through the obstacles and challenges that arise on a daily basis.

Opportunity: Make a list of your accomplishments, derailers, and disappointments.

Lesson #18 - Recognize and Focus on Your Challenges

Hi Ray!

It's been a productive and relaxing weekend. For some reason, it was easier than normal to keep a good balance! There are tons of updates from PLP, classes, GMAT, and apartment hunting. We can talk about them all in the morning.

I know the next two weeks will be even more high stress than normal for a couple of reasons, so the next two weeks I will need to be VERY careful and strategic to keep the balance that has been present recently!

See you in the morning!

Alexia

Ray,

The past two days have been crazy for me! My to do list is a bit longer than normal and pressures for one incredibly hard and stressful class have had me very focused to keep everything in my life balanced despite the added stress! Last night I actually fell asleep reading! I just finished my RA on call rounds and am off to get a good night's sleep so I can get a fresh start tomorrow and hopefully have an even more productive day. I can't wait for our meeting on Monday... I have a lot of other little updates to catch you up on!

Talk to you soon!

Alexia

Ray,

After a pretty productive day reading for classes and working on PLP tasks, I worked desk. At desk, I did some research on the exam dates. The GMAT has tests available at least once a week (mostly with multiple times a day) around the DFW area throughout February, March and April of 2014. In addition, this afternoon, I went and picked up the newest Kaplan GMAT prep book so I have that to begin working through. I think I may set aside some time this weekend to either try and take a practice test to see where I am at or at least begin looking at the material to see how familiar or foreign it all looks to me. Hopefully that will help give me a better idea as to where to go from there in regards to the GMAT.

As for the LSAT, there are not as many test days! There is one in February which would be way to soon! The next one would be June 9th. That is the date I will be planning to take it on. If I should decide to retake it or in case some emergency happens in June, I looked up the following date which would be in October. I will be going to the pre-law advisor in the morning to get more information and direction, so I should be able to have a plan in place by next Monday! See you at the meeting tomorrow!

Alexia

Alexia's Goal Evaluation in March 2014

Professional Learning and Development Goals	On Track?	Comments
Goal 1: Be fully prepared for the GMAT. Shoot for score: 710 (University of Chicago's median is 720 - ranked #1 B-School by Business Weekly)	No	I am honestly not where I want to be, but I am refocusing. I pushed back the date of the GMAT to April 12th to help keep me from becoming too overwhelmed.
Goal 2: Be fully prepared for the LSAT. Shoot for score: 170 (University of Chicago's median is 171 - ranked #5 for Law Schools)	Yes	Not really started yet, but not meant to be started yet. Classes for the LSAT will start April 15th.

Personal Goals	On Track?	Comments
Goal 1: Improve work life balance techniques	No	Still not 100% successful, but still doing better than before.
Goal 2: Maintain 4.0 GPA	Yes	It's a bit more of a struggle than normal given my overwhelming schedule but it is still possible!

Lesson: Recognize and focus on your challenges.

Notice the specific goals and not all of them were on track. You have to be honest with yourself and recognize what is working and what is not so you can get back on track.

Also, notice how she worked to find out the median score for the University of Chicago. She didn't guess or hope. She looked up the score and then set that as her goal with plenty of time to make it happen. She then measured her progress using practice tests and made adjustments. The measurement allowed her to gauge her level of success and make adjustments. In the case of the GMAT, she moved back the date so she would have more time to study.

As you review your goals you will find areas where you can improve and make changes. Focus on those challenge areas and work to improve them. Often we get discouraged or get too busy with the stress and chaos of life. Don't let that distract you from reaching your goals, especially the difficult goals. Be confident in your ability to move forward and make progress, one small step at a time. Recognize and appreciate the success at each step and build your confidence over time. Turn your challenges into your successes.

Opportunity: Review your goals and list three challenges you are facing and your solutions to overcome those challenges.

Create Plans and Implement

with Discipline

Lesson #19 - Make a Plan

From Alexia's Journal: *I dream of a very productive week! I will give my undivided attention to my work and get well ahead so I can have a FUN, RELAXING weekend in College Station.*

Ray,

Today was a smooth transition back into work and classes! After work and class, I made a plan for this week and got some RA work done. I got a workout in and am now off to bed!

Have a wonderful rest of the week!

Alexia

Lesson: Make a Plan.

Leaders make plans. Many people romanticize leadership as the charismatic person who just naturally knows what to do next.

Although the "fly by the seat of your pants" and "instinctively know what to do" type of leadership might exist, it is not very common. Leadership can be as simple as being the person who takes time to make a plan. To be a better leader start by thinking about the big picture and taking time to organize your tasks and priorities so the next steps are clear. As the "organized person" you could become the de facto leader because you won't be overwhelmed by the hundreds of swirling options. If you take the time to group or categorize those options and create a plan you can help get the team started.

Many people believe they are not the most organized person on the team. As a leader, your plan may be as simple as finding the most organized person and working with him or her to help you organize next steps and actions, prior to the team meeting. In other words, make a plan to recruit help in making a plan.

A few other benefits of being an organized leader:

- Your team will have more confidence in someone who is clear on next steps.
- Your team will become more cohesive as they accomplish small tasks together on the way to a larger goal.
- Your team will begin to work independently as they create successes with your short term plan and can begin to visualize the long term potential.

Opportunity: Make a Plan for Your Next Team Meeting
1. Pull your list of goals and priorities from the previous chapters.
2. Brainstorm a list of actions you should take to reach those goals.

3. Put the list in sequential order. What has to happen first before anything else can be done? What has to happen second? For items that don't have a natural sequential order, but them in order of priority. Largest priorities first.

4. For each action, write down the name of the person on the team who would be the best leader for that action. Who has the most interest or relevant experience and knowledge?

5. Take your plan to the meeting and offer it to the team. Ask for volunteers and recommend the people on your list. Explain to the team why they would be best suited for the role.

Opportunity: Make a Plan for Your Week

1. What are your goals and priorities?

2. What do you have to accomplish or attend to this week?

3. Put time on your calendar for each activity.

4. Color code the activities by level of importance.

5. Remember to leave open time for the unexpected.

6. Follow your calendar and see how much you get done.

Alexia with Friends and Family

Lesson #20 - Daily Effort to Reach Your Goals

Ray,

Tonight after work I started updating my résumé because work needs an updated copy before the official end of the internship. Did a 30 minute workout and am now writing in my journals before bed!

Alexia

Ray,

Today I spent some hours working on McKesson projects, made sure I was on top of all my school work for the week and ahead on readings for all my classes, had some me time and friends time, and am now done with RA on call close down procedures and am off to do my journals and head to bed!

Alexia

PS. I plan to call a few offices tomorrow to set up times to meet with the different advisors/professors that we discussed and built into my goals. Hopefully they will be pretty available with it being the first few weeks of classes!

Ray,

It's been a productive day between classes, RA Programs, getting responses from the law schools and a few McKesson hours worth of work done! I just finished some me time and am now off to bed! Talk to you soon!

Alexia

PS. The missing person returned this morning, so that's good news too!

Ray,

<u>Today I talked to Rachel and the remaining SDs about the new SD situation. It looks like we are headed toward bringing them on board fully!</u>

<u>Also, today was the career fair. We got an early start on recruiting and even gained some new possible mentors/sponsors for the program!</u>

I just finished an assignment due tomorrow at noon and, ironically, when I opened my email, I saw my professor emailed me that there have been some issues accessing the online assignment and we now have 24 extra hours to complete it... I may have stayed up longer than planned to complete it but at least I am ahead now!

<u>Overall it's been a good day!</u>

Have a wonderful night and I will talk to you tomorrow!

Alexia

Ray,

<u>Everything that absolutely needed to get done this week has.</u> I have three online quizzes due by this weekend that I plan to take tonight but the reading for them is already done. In addition, I have a huge project I need to start working on this weekend. I am hoping to get the majority of it done. And then, in addition, <u>I want to get ahead on some readings for the upcoming week.</u>

I am not behind by any means <u>I just really need to use this weekend to keep comfortably ahead of everything!</u>

Thanks,

Alexia

Ray,

Today, I got to sleep in which was needed! I felt reenergized this morning when I rolled out of bed!

I spoke with my AIS professor (the class I will need to put a bit more effort into to ensure I get an A) and he said as I am studying between now and the final to create a list of technical terms I don't fully understand, questions I may have, and any topics that I am not quite understanding too well and that we can meet before the final to talk through those points and ensure I understand them before going in to take the final.

As for personal goal achievements today, I had some me time, some friends time, and some exercise time.

I hope you have a wonderful Friday and a great weekend! Talk to you soon!

Alexia

Ray,

Today, I had a productive day at work! We wrapped up a bit early and then I actually got a chance to start looking into apartments for next year!

This evening, I had some "girls time" with three friends. We went to get manicures and pedicures and then had dinner!

Afterward, I came back and was more productive for my classes.

I'm in a great mood and am ready for a productive weekend!!!

Talk to you soon!

Alexia

Hey Ray!

So today I slept in a bit and then met with Tina again this morning to talk about her scorecard and make sure we are both on the same page for next semester. Tied with that, we did create a simple action plan to make sure she stays connected to the program. I can give you a full update Monday!

I also met with my systems professor because that last project that I got a 246/300 (or an 82 percentage) on was all due to my writing one digit in one number wrong when I copied it over to the formal trial balance worksheet.... Conceptually, all my work was correct and all my numbers added up right. I made one stupid little mistake that caused follow through errors which resulted in my 82%..... Boy was I mad at myself when I figure that out!!!

From meeting with him however, he did make the deal with me that if I get a perfect grade on the Peachtree project, we will talk about getting some points back on the SUA to help bring my grade up. Thankfully, this project is a bit simpler because its computerized and helps eliminate errors like I made in the SUA. In addition, it has check figures in the material to see if I have the right numbers before moving on. So far, no errors!

In addition, we spoke a little more about setting up a one-on-one after the thanksgiving break to help review for the final. The conversation with him just reinforced for me that I am not settling for a B! There is still hope for an A!

It's already a longer email than normal so I won't bother you with too many more details of my day! However, I did have some me time today which was much needed! In addition, I put on a program at the hall tonight because residents wanted to learn how to two-step so it was three hours of non-stop cardio activity! In addition, I did a little personal workout after just for me!

Again, sorry for the super long email!

I hope you have a wonderful weekend!

Talk to you soon!

Alexia

Ray,

After work and class I did a little work out, got some homework done and completed some tasks for RA!

It's been a productive day!

Talk to you tomorrow!

Alexia

Ray,

Today has been a lot of class, PLP office hours, and working on my project. I have one more closing procedure to do and I am all done! I am so close which has me in a great mood heading to bed!

Have a wonderful day tomorrow!

Alexia

Lesson: Daily effort to reach your goals

It is easy to walk out of class or leave work and just assume that you are done for the day. You did your work, you put in the hours, and you are tired and ready to relax. But finding a few minutes to put in a little extra effort to get a few things done that move you closer to your goals and dreams will be the difference between living an unfulfilled life and finding happiness and success. An even better solution is to schedule an extra 15 minutes in the morning, to ensure you put in that little extra effort before the day overwhelms you. Spending 15 minutes in the morning to put in a little extra effort towards reaching your goals, gives you a feeling of accomplishment all day.

Many people get stuck looking at the big goal they will eventually accomplish instead of the small steps they can take each day. It is easy to become overwhelmed with everything that has to be accomplished to reach your goal or to put off getting started until you have a large chunk of time to focus and plan. But reaching your goals is about daily effort. It is about finding a little time each day to move you one step farther along. Believe it or not, reaching a goal is not what brings people happiness and success. Reaching the goal is almost anti-climatic. Your happiness and success comes from the accomplishment and confidence you create each day. It comes from your belief in your ability to consistently put in the effort that will lead to a positive outcome.

That is why it is important to focus on your effort daily. Your happiness and success comes not from reaching your final goal, but in fighting daily to get through life and accomplish a little bit each day. When you feel overwhelmed and ready to quit, especially when you are 90% there, stop and take a minute to breathe and then take on one day or one hour at a time. Do the best you can and take satisfaction in your effort, rather than worrying about the outcome, which you may or may not be able to control. To be a great leader, put in daily effort and accomplish something every day. Become an example of how baby steps lead to big accomplishments.

Opportunity: Spend 15 minutes each morning identifying a few things that you need to do that day to reach your goals.

Lesson #21 – Make Each Day Productive

Ray,

Today was a productive day full of staff bonding, training, meeting with Rachel to catch up on PLP things and accomplishing some McKesson work tonight. I'm now doing journals and am off to bed!

Alexia

Ray,

I had a very busy productive day between RA and PLP! I accomplished A LOT in the last 24 hours! And I am now off to bed!!

Alexia

Ray,

I had some me time this morning and continued with some exercise this morning. Had RA training and fun relaxing activities today. And after tonight's SD meeting, I am caught up with PLP stuff for the next week. I just did my journals and I am off to bed!

Alexia

Ray,

I completed all my stuff for today, had a successful first PLP SD meeting and Wednesday meeting and am now off to bed!

Alexia

Ray,

<u>Today has been a good day!</u> I went to breakfast and got a massage with Shannon! Then we had a long but productive student director meeting. I also got a few cases read between SD meeting and member meeting. I got a little exercising in and then did nothing but GMAT problems while working desk tonight!

I just finished up my me time and journaling and am now off to bed!

Talk to you soon!

Alexia

Lesson: Make each day productive.

Are you making progress on your goals every day? Are you accomplishing the things you need to get done, or are you caught up in the chaos of life? In one of the emails above, Alexia started the day with a good breakfast and then spent time nurturing relationships and taking care of herself. Then she had a productive meeting with her team, the Professional Leadership Program Student Directors. She got her homework done, fit in some exercise to stay healthy, and went to work at her second job as a Resident Assistant and found time to study for her GMAT to help her prepare for her goal to get a combined MBA/Law degree. Finally, she ended the day with some journaling and making sure she got plenty of sleep. Alexia was not super human. She was organized, disciplined and committed to her goals. Anyone, including you, can have this kind of productive day. Set your goals, clarify your priorities, and create the discipline to follow through.

Success and leadership are not a result of one great accomplishment or one big action. They are a result of lots of productive days doing the right things related to your goals day in and day out, over and over again. It has to become routine and habit to know what your priorities are and to make sure you create a little progress on those priorities each day. The big wins are almost anti-climactic because they come after many routine days of taking the actions that are moving you towards accomplishment of that big goal. Don't wait for the right opportunity to be a leader. Don't wait for success to happen. Long term happiness is created by lots of productive days strung together that lead to success, not by one big win in a lucky moment. Make leadership and success a part of your daily routine. Make them habits that happen every day and are an integrated part of your life.

Opportunity: Evaluate how productive was your day today and determine how can you make tomorrow more productive?

Lesson #22 - There Will Be Chaos. Learn to Roll with It.

Ray,

Sorry! I thought about that this morning. We have had a program going on in the hall all week, Assassins, and every evening there have been discipline things to deal with... They are getting way to crazy and disobedient with the rules! That is preoccupying some of my time combined with a big midterm I took today and the big project due next week. I have been scatter brained and falling asleep as soon as I sit in bed! I have even fallen asleep before getting to my journals, or even while studying, a few of these past nights. I have still been sleeping seven to eight hours and getting my exercises in. I usually am able to squeeze some extra me time in on top of what I have scheduled weekly, but this week I haven't found much of that extra time.

Otherwise things are going well! Just staying VERY busy!

Hope all has been well with you! How did your meetings with Wayne and Marty go?

Thanks,

Alexia

As a Resident Assistant for an on-campus dorm, Alexia and her team had to be available for whatever might come up with students who are fighting through the pressures and challenges of making their grades, figuring out who they are, and deciding what they will do with the rest of their lives. Many of the most dramatic events occur in the middle of the night and there is not an opportunity for planning.

Hey Ray,

Unfortunately, I had to deal with a missing person situation for quite some time tonight. I just wrapped up writing my report for housing and am finally able to lay down for bed! I did have some me time today and some exercise time. I did my journals and am off to bed. Good night.

Alexia

Ray,

I had to deal with more crazy on call situations tonight so I am just getting to bed but I did get a nap today and some me time so I'm feeling pretty good and pretty refreshed!

Alexia

Ray,

Unfortunately some RAs were dealing with two different students in crises/upset student situations tonight. Because of those, I am unfortunately just now getting showered and ready for bed.

I will update you more on my meeting with Professor Staff and her advice for my career going forward on Monday when we meet.

Have a good night (or I should say morning!)

Alexia

Ray,

Today I had plenty of rest and me time to help hold off the cold that I have been feeling coming on. I am now all done with on call stuff. <u>Hopefully I won't have any more pages in the middle of the night!</u>

Alexia

Ray,

You already got a brief overview of the RA staff meeting and the meeting with the pre-law advisor. Everything seems to be in a better/ more hopeful situation than before, so that's a plus! I can give you more details and we can talk through an action plan on Monday.

<u>A bit of devastating news tonight... My laptop gave me issues turning on last night and when I called tech support tonight they said my lap top is no longer under warranty.</u> They were able to tell me what the most likely issue is, the motherboard, based on my description of the problem and advised me to get it checked at a Best Buy to confirm the issue. Downside is they no longer make my laptop so even if I can confirm the issue, parts probably are scarce and potentially costly, if even still available. The whole situation will put a strain on my always staying productive between classes and commitments, <u>but I will have to find a way to make do until I can resolve the issue!... Yet another curve ball and life lesson in learning to be adaptable!</u>

I also got some exercise in today so between it all, I have had about all my energy sucked out of me for today! So, I am off to finish my journals, crash, and sleep in a bit tomorrow morning!

Have a good night and I will talk to you tomorrow!

Alexia

Lesson: There will be chaos. Learn to roll with it.

"I am sorry to say so,
but, sadly, it's true
that Bang-ups
and Hang-ups
can happen to you."

Dr. Seuss

No matter how well you plan or how organized you are; the chaos of life can and will interfere. Our computer breaks down, our car won't start, or someone on the team doesn't deliver as promised. When these challenges arise, you can worry, scream, and stomp your feet; or you can calmly assess the situation and determine what to do next. You can focus on the disruption and challenge or you can focus on getting back on track. People want to follow leaders who are calm in the face of new challenges and unexpected roadblocks. They want leaders who have or can create a Plan B without having an emotional meltdown. They will look for you to remain confident, adjust, and adapt, so they can remain confident and flexible. As a leader, accept that unexpected challenges will disrupt your best plans at the worst times. Take a moment to feel the frustration. Then quickly consider the impacts, evaluate your options, and create a list of next steps. Stay calm and quickly adapt to those challenges. The chaos of life is going to happen. You can let it ruin your plans and your day, or you can adapt and change, and be happy anyway.

Opportunity: Evaluate how well you are adapting to the chaos that interrupts your plans.

Lesson #23 – Have a Plan B?

Hi Ray!

Today has been very interesting! I had a slow start this morning when Suzanne and I went to breakfast and she accidentally locked her keys in her car! I had planned on being productive in between the SD meeting and PLP meeting...but I ran into challenges there as well!!! But after the meetings, I got a lot of school and RA work done! Of course there is still A LOT to do, but I am now off to try and get some rest!

Alexia

Ray,

A Student Director resigned this morning. Considering our talk this morning, I thought you might find this interesting. In addition, I wanted you to know because the actions and plans moving forward may become a big topic for us at our meetings.

In addition, I got some very scary news from my advising department. Apparently it is no longer possible to do a dual degree in finance and accounting due to two classes no longer being available and that causing too much overlap between the degrees. There may be a way around it but I have to speak with the department advisors to be sure. Hopefully it works out! If not, I need to rework my plans for the next few years here. Talk to you soon,

Alexia

Ray,

I am meeting with Rachel tomorrow to discuss what to do from here. My guess is we will look at bringing in a new SD, someone who applied last year and will be a good fit. In the mean time though, I need to figure out who would be able to take on the extra work, get it done, and not be overwhelmed with their existing tasks. This week will be interesting.

Alexia

Ray,

Today I took a shorter day at work, went to the student meeting, and then came right home and got productive! I completed my review and got a good amount of studying done for accounting. I planned on getting up and reviewing a bit more in the morning before the exam, but it looks like we might be closed tomorrow. An email already went out but the website still just says frozen rain advisory and we have not yet received the eagle alert. If classes are cancelled tomorrow, I will have an entire day to be productive!!! If not I will stick to my current plan.

Talk to you soon,

Alexia

Lesson: Have a plan B?

The chaos of life will interfere with your best laid plans. Don't be surprised when it happens. It is not helpful to become angry or frustrated and let your mood derail your energy and productivity. Pause and take a breath. Realize how frustrating it is, and then move on to Plan B. Plan B is your alternate route to accomplishing the same goal or task. Implementing your Plan B will usually require you to identify and adjust your highest priority activities and make sure they still get done. Then move your lower priority items to other days on your calendar. It is great if you know your Plan B ahead of time, but sometimes you have to make it up on the spot or work through it over time. Think calmly about how to handle the current situation and take action there. Then move to your highest priorities and what you have to get done. Finally, shuffle the lower priorities as needed. Stay calm and take the interruptions in stride, and always have a rough Plan B in your back pocket.

Opportunity: Have a plan for what you would do if you dropped and broke your computer or phone.

FYI – Alexia's Plan B worked out.

Ray,

<u>Thankfully today I got the substitution form approved to be able to still double major in finance and accounting!</u>

The SD meeting today went pretty well. There are some topics I am eager to talk to you about and get your advice on Monday, but overall, things are going well.

I'm off to bed!

Alexia

Get Organized

Lesson #24 - Being Organized Helps You Start Strong

First Day of the Semester

Ray,

Today has been quite the day! Besides a few morning sessions and opening the hall today, I gathered and prepared all my books and materials for the semester, signed up for the March 3rd GMAT, and signed up for the June 9th LSAT. I am feeling pretty good about today!

I just finished journaling and am off to get some rest before what will hopefully be another very productive day tomorrow!

Talk to you soon!

Alexia

Lesson: Being organized helps you start strong.

The next time you start a project, school semester, or job, you can walk in flustered and worried or you can take the time to prepare and organize so that you begin strong and confident. Take some time to do a little research and planning up front. Clarify your priorities and what you want to get done on the first day. Start with a rough outline of what you want to accomplish in the first week. Rather than worrying and fretting about what you don't know, make a plan around what you do know. Make a list of questions you need answered or a list of topics you want to learn more about. Getting organized will help you start with confidence and curiosity. It will help you approach new adventures with strength and leadership rather than fear and trepidation.

You can't eliminate the fear of the unknown in a new setting. You can only build confidence in your ability to face it and survive. The fear is there to help your body prepare for the unfamiliar. It is a signal that you are doing something exciting and outside of your comfort zone. Get organized to help reduce the fear and set you on the right track, but don't expect or even try to eliminate all your fear. Embrace it and let it motivate you to become better.

Opportunity: Don't wait for a new job or a new semester. Monday is the beginning of a new day. Get organized so you can begin the week with confidence.

Lesson #25 - Life is Too Busy Not to Be Organized

Ray,

Today has been a busy day! I woke up and spent the morning reviewing for my exam and working on some homework. I then had classes and PLP SD office hours, came home long enough to eat and get a little workout in and then had to work the front desk.

In between it all I was able to spend time getting things organized and taken care of for PLP, was able to work out a plan for GMAT and LSAT testing, and got some more homework taken care of. I am now exhausted and am off to do my journals and head to bed!

Talk to you soon!

Alexia

Lesson: Life is too busy not to be organized.

One of the biggest challenges for leaders and for life in general is that we are all "too busy to be less busy." We have so many things that we want to accomplish in a day that we feel we don't have time to stop and plan. There is just no time as we run from one activity to the next. Yet the key to successful leadership is forcing yourself to pause for a few minutes to create your plan. Get clear on what you want to accomplish. What are your priorities and therefore needs to be done first? Where does everything fit into your schedule, and therefore what might have to be dropped because there is not enough time? The busier you become, the more important it is to pause for a few minutes and get organized. It will help you clarify your next steps, understand your priorities, and reduce your stress; and you will accomplish more with less effort.

Opportunity: Put a time on your calendar tomorrow when you will stop and get organized. For most people it is first thing in the morning, but it could be also around lunch, an afternoon break, or preparing for tomorrow as you wrap up today.

Lesson #26 - Keep Track of Who Signed up for What

At every meeting and through email when we weren't having meetings, Alexia would ask each of us about our deliverables. She usually took notes on the agendas and wrote down what everyone was responsible for. She always knew what we needed to do and checked in to confirm it had been done. We felt accountable to deliver for her each week. Several of our team members had other priorities and if Alexia hadn't stayed on top of it, they would not have put in the time to work on the PLP stuff.   *Austin Hatcher*

Lesson: Keep track of who signed up for what.

A simple step for being an organized leader is writing down the actions each person has agreed to take and by when they will be completed. This small task keeps the teams on track and helps ensure the team is actually accomplishing something vs. just meeting, talking, and coming up with great ideas, but then not getting anything done. As a leader, "Inspect what you expect." If you expect a team member to accomplish a task, you have to inspect whether they are on track for completion. There will be a few members who don't need the reminders, but the rest will welcome your help.

Opportunity: Determine how you will you track assignments at your next meeting.

Lesson #27 – Keep a "To-Do" List

Ray,

Today was the first day of classes for me. I got A LOT done in PLP office hours today and feel confident about kicking off the semester with our SD meeting and member meeting tomorrow! In addition, I got a final approval from Central Housing today to take an LSAT prep course. After that, I registered and secured my spot in the class I wanted!

In between it all, <u>I got a lot of little things crossed off of my to do list</u>! It has been a bit of a long day, but a pretty productive day as well! Talk to you soon!

Alexia

Ray,

This weekend was exactly what I needed! I was able to spend some time with my friends and my family, as well as get some work done! <u>I was able to spend some time getting my to do list put together and making a plan for the week so that I can get as much done as possible</u>! In addition, I was able to spend some quality me time and tons of playing with my dog time! I am feeling very refreshed and ready to go for the week! See you in the morning!

Alexia

Ray,

Today has been quite a long day for not having much on my schedule. <u>I have gotten a handful of things crossed off my to-do list, but I do have a lot left</u>. It will have to make for a productive weekend! I'm tired and now off to bed! Can't wait for our meeting on Monday... It feels like its been forever!

Alexia

Ray,

Today I had a very productive day at work, productive class and a pretty productive night as well. I had some me time and some friends time and also got a workout in. I still have a lot on my to do list for the week but I feel like I'm at a good spot as of now! I'm off to bed!

Goodnight,

Alexia

Lesson: Keep a "to-do" list.

If you want to get things done, you will need a "to-do" list. If you want to be a leader, you need items on your "to-do" list related to accomplishing your goals and the goals of the team. You want activities that will matter and make a difference in your life and the lives of others. Review your "to-do" list; if it includes things like "buy milk" and "stop by the bookstore," then it is good you have those items captured. But what you really need is a list of the activities that are most important to reaching your goals and helping the team reach its goals. Don't just think about what you have to do, but think about what is the most important thing you can be doing? Look at your "to-do" list and add the actions that will move your goals forward. Make sure those are prioritized so you get them done first. Then add all of the other smaller items swirling around in your head. But be sure to mark them a lower priority and fit them into the schedule vs. spending your time on the lower priority items and never getting to the activities that will make you successful and happy.

One important note; make positive relationships one of your top priorities. Nurturing positive relationships is an investment in your happiness and success.

Opportunity: Create a "to-do" list. Put a priority level next to each item. Do the high priority items first.

Activity: Schedule your to-do list

Make a list of things you need to do tomorrow and schedule each one on your calendar to hold yourself accountable. Make sure your most important activities get the highest priority times and the most cushion in your calendar. Check your calendar often and stick to your scheduled times.

At the end of the day, tomorrow, review your success. Check each item and confirm whether you were able to complete it or not. Did you schedule enough time to complete the activity? Did you schedule enough transition time and down time? Honestly evaluate your progress. Did you get side tracked by something unexpected? Was it more important than what you had originally planned or just more urgent?

Your schedule should remain flexible, so don't worry about being perfect and never missing a scheduled activity. It is more about creating a habit, learning to budget enough time, and making sure the highest priority activities don't get replaced by the lower priority activities.

Lesson #28 - Leaders Take Good Notes

Plain and simple Alexia always took great notes. She had a system that allowed her to take great notes in a timely manner. She also organized herself in a way that she could find those notes at ease for reference. I remember looking over and wondering, "What is she getting that I am not" or just plainly being impressed at her organized knowledge management system. Her notes were a reflection of her passion to learn everything she could. "Alexia = a learning sponge"   *Austin Hatcher*

Lesson: Leaders take good notes.

How many meetings have you been in with great discussion and great collaboration but no progress? The next time you meet, which might be a week or even a month later, you struggle to remember the discussion and end up re-hashing the same points from the last meeting. You have that feeling that there was some great learning or idea that came out of the last meeting, but you just can't remember what it was. Practice taking notes. Highlight key points and action items. Taking notes will help you learn and remember. Notes become a great starting point for the team to kick-off the next meeting. They help the team maintain continuity and keep making progress rather than re-hashing old discussions over and over again. There are a lot of things that happen in a day. Trying to remember everything important creates stress and takes up space in your brain that could be used for thinking, planning, and adapting to the chaos. Taking notes will help you think more clearly and gives you a reference point to confirm your next steps.

Opportunity: Assign someone to take notes at the next meeting. Write down next steps, with owners and dates.

Alexia at the University of North Texas Leadership Program

Lesson #29 - Do Your Work in 90 Minute Sprints

with15 Minute Breaks

Ray,

Since we met this morning, my day has been mainly McKesson work, like most Mondays. However, I did try and use the 15 minutes breaks you suggested when I was working on homework. The listening to music, taking a walk, and stretching/exercising seemed to refresh me the most. I just finished my "me" time, focusing on what some stressors are in my life, completed my journals and am now off to bed.

Have a good night!

Alexia

Lesson: Do your work in 90-minute sprints with 15-minute breaks.

One of the most common solutions people pursue when being overwhelmed with things to do is sitting down and just plowing through their list without breaks. But research has shown that we can't be productive for 5 or 6 hours straight because we need time to refresh and renew our energy. We can actually maximize our productivity by working in 90-minute sprints with 15-minute breaks in between. Take the time to focus and be super productive in that 90 minutes and then take 15 minutes to walk around and get some fresh air, a drink of water, or a light snack.

Quick Tip: One challenge with the 15-minute breaks is that they often last much longer because it is hard to discipline ourselves to get back to work. During your break don't watch TV or start anything that will absorb more than 15 minutes. Just take time to breathe and walk around. Be diligent about sitting back down and starting the next project after your 15 minutes are up.

Opportunity: Schedule three 90-minute work sessions on your calendar with 15-minute breaks between each one. Try to work without distractions for the full 90 minutes.

Lesson #30 - Set Expectations and Keep Commitments

Ray,

Today was a very long day. Besides classes, I got some reading and research done and spent some time on the GMAT material. In addition, today was one of my exercise days. I just did my journaling and am now off to bed.

I will be heading home to Houston tomorrow after work. I plan to be back Sunday evening, but if dad still needs an extra hand, I may stay through Monday. I'll give you an update on Sunday.

Have a wonderful weekend!

Alexia

Hi Ray!

I wanted to be sure to let you know before Monday that I am out of town. Suzanne and I are currently in Atlanta checking out the city and Georgia State University. Tomorrow we are headed to Orlando and then Monday morning Suzanne starts her Disney internship and I head home!

Just wanted to give you an update! Hopefully we can do dinner or something soon!

Alexia

Lesson: Set expectations and keep commitments.

As a leader you will have lots of meetings and commitments. Any number of circumstances will create havoc with your schedule. Make an extra effort to communicate and keep people informed. Let others know ahead of time if you might miss a commitment. Apologize for the commitments you do miss and offer to reschedule. Don't go silent because you get too busy, you are overscheduled, or you never really wanted to meet them in the first place. Own your commitments, consider the impact of your absence to the other people, and take responsibility for using their time wisely. Leaders are responsible and dependable. They set expectations and keep their commitments.

Opportunity: Look at your schedule for tomorrow. See what commitments you are in danger of missing or being late for. Contact the people who will be affected and set expectations, reschedule, or cancel.

Take Care of Yourself

Lesson #31 - Make Time for Yourself

Ray,

This weekend was exactly what I needed! I was able to spend some time with my friends and my family, as well as get some work done! I was able to spend some time getting my to do list put together and making a plan for the week so that I can get as much done as possible! In addition, I was able to spend some quality "me" time and tons of playing with my dog time! I am feeling very refreshed and ready to go for the week!

See you in the morning!

Alexia

Ray,

Today has been a good day! I got up and had my classes then PLP office hours where I got a lot done! (I also have the jump drive Rachel wants me to give you with a copy of your presentation on it.) Afterwards, I had some productive homework time! I continued to try your tips (changing scenery, taking breaks filled with movement, fresh air, and me time, etc). It seems to really be helping me stay productive when I'm working and relaxed during my breaks. And getting out of my room I think has helped my productivity the most!

To add to good news, I have breakfast plans and a massage with Shannon in the morning! So hopefully, tomorrow will be an even better day! Talk to you soon!

Alexia

Lesson: Make time for yourself.

One of the keys to being a good leader is setting a good example and taking care of yourself. Unfortunately, none of us has an unlimited supply of energy. We need to pause and renew. We need to pull back from the world and take care of ourselves so we can be prepared and full of the energy we need to help others. Make time each day to focus on your health. Take time to renew your physical, mental, emotional, and spiritual energy. Go for a walk or call a friend. Rather than sitting at your desk all day, get up and take a walk or find a change of scenery. Go outside and get some fresh air. Take time for a pleasant meal and conversation with friends and family. Take a few moments to contemplate and write down your dreams or the things in life you are grateful for. Make time for yourself to renew your energy and you will find an abundance of energy to lead others.

Opportunity: Schedule some "me" time.

Lesson #32 - Listen to Your Body

Alexia,

Are you getting 7 to 8 hours of sleep per night?

Ray

Ray,

Most days yes! The times dealing with an RA situation, or whatever the case may be, has me up later than I probably should be, I just tend to wake up a bit later in the morning. There have been maybe two or three exceptions since I moved back to Denton, but that's it.

Alexia

Ray

I think my body is just still trying to adjust to being around so many other people and so many more germs than its been used to all summer. I think that's why I have been feeling like a cold is coming on for a little while now. That's also probably why yesterday I fell asleep so early and slept till my body felt rested. This tends to happen in some way every fall move in.

Alexia

Ray,

Thankfully I haven't felt the cold coming on any worse lately, but in the past few days, I have had a few random times that I have gotten very hot, light headed and, according to everyone around me, very pale... I'm not sure what that's about but I am trying to drink plenty of water to stay hydrated and take vitamins daily to help my immune system stay strong.

Alexia

Ray,

I first woke up this morning around nine and tried to be productive but still was feeling tired and unfocused so I decided to let myself sleep a little longer. Once I got back up about two hours later, I felt pretty good and was able to be very focused and productive for a while without getting distracted or side tracked. I was able to focus much longer than in the past few days so that's a good sign! I haven't felt faint yet today, but that seems to be more likely to happen in the evenings so I will let you know later if it happens today or not. Hopefully with the extra rest it won't!

See you in the morning!

Alexia

Hey Ray!

Sorry for all the emails today. Just wanted to give you an update that I have felt good today! No faintness and no sudden or unexplained heat waves, so that's a good thing! I am done with all my RA on call duties for the night and am off to bed!

Talk to you soon!

Alexia

Ray,

Today was a great and productive day at work! By the time I got home, however, I had a terrible headache. Therefore, I wasn't as productive as I had hoped to be tonight. *I did take a nap and get the headache to a manageable point and got a few things accomplished. I'm hoping with some extra rest, it will be gone by tomorrow morning!*

Have a wonderful night!

Alexia

Ray,

Today was a pretty productive day. Thankfully, I was feeling a lot better today. My headache was very minimal and I got a lot done! I had some me time this morning so that was great! Hope your week is going well!

Alexia

Ray,

So this morning I woke up with my throat hurting very badly. It hurt to cough, swallow, talk, everything. So I went to the health center and I found out I have tonsillitis. *So I got a prescription, have drank lots of tea, have taken a few naps, and overall am having to take it extra easy until I can shake this! What a crazy time for it to hit me!*

On the upside, this weekend's GMAT class was cancelled since I was the only one signed up. Instead they upgraded me to the online, on demand course with more instruction time and therefore more detailed practice for me to work through over the break. *Therefore, I can afford to take it extra easy this week and focus on recovering.*

Talk to you soon,

Alexia

Hi Ray!

Today has been a busy day considering no work or school. I have been studying a lot and was able to finally get out of the hall a bit (which was a very refreshing change of pace!).

There has been a lot of resting, studying, and dealing with cabin fevered residents this weekend! Thankfully, with the relaxed schedule these past few days, I am starting to feel like I have fully recovered from the tonsillitis... Just in time for finals!

I just finished journaling and am now off to bed!

Talk to you soon!

Alexia

Lesson: Listen to your body.

Listen to what your body is telling you. It gives you warnings before it finally breaks down and puts a halt to everything you are doing. You can't lead or get anything else done when you are sick and your body shuts down. Listen to the hints and interrupt your schedule to sleep a little extra, drink plenty of water, eat the right foods, and if necessary go see a doctor. It is better to take a little time now, than to be forced by your body to stop everything so you can get well again.

Opportunity: Slow down when you feel sick, and get well.

"There is deep wisdom within our very flesh, if we can only come to our senses and feel it."   Elizabeth A. Behnke

Lesson #33 - Make Time to Exercise

Hey Ray!

This morning I got up and tried just the 5-10 minute workout to start the day and I had a pretty productive day! I have gotten a lot off my checklist as well as I had two one hour breaks for some friends time. Then tonight I did a full 30 minute workout and now I'm off to bed to get a good night's rest in preparation for another productive day tomorrow!

Alexia

Ray

I have still been exercising but not every other day like I was a few weeks ago. I do need to get back into that habit.

Alexia

Hey Ray!

Not much has changed since my update earlier, but we did have some volleyball games tonight that kept me active and helped relieve a lot of stress from this week! It was good to do something not school or work related!

I'm now off to do my journals and head to bed!

Alexia

Lesson: Make time to exercise.

Make time for exercise. It reduces stress, reduces depression, gives you energy and helps you live longer.

One of our biggest challenges with exercise is that we feel like we just don't have the time. But not making the time actually hurts our mental state and our confidence. If we can begin an exercise program, even just a few minutes a day a few days per week, we will feel healthier and mentally stronger.

Exercise gives you more energy and provides a mental and emotional break from your daily stress. It gives you time to think and solve nagging challenges. Exercise improves the brain's ability to process information. Overall, exercise helps you think more clearly, feel more confident, and be more energetic, all of which help you become a better leader.

Opportunity: Put 15 minutes on your calendar each day to walk down the block. You don't have to go far; just get yourself moving on a regular basis.

Lesson #34 - Get Enough Sleep

Ray,

This weekend has been a bit crazy! I was busier from an RA standpoint than I expected, thankfully only administratively and not disciplinary like you might expect on a homecoming weekend! I have had exercise time, plenty of me time, <u>and a lot of sleep, which was relaxing!</u> In addition, I got a good amount of school work done! See you soon!

Alexia

Ray,

Today I took some extra me time! It's been a long week and I knew I could use some relaxing! I also exercised and got another section of my project done. <u>I am now off to bed to try and get a good night's rest!</u> Talk to you soon!

Alexia

Ray,

I hope you had a safe flight today! I have been staying very productive with work and my school work! I had a pretty relaxing day working from home and all. Nothing to stressful happened so that's a big plus! I took some me time and exercised some as well. <u>Now I am off to bed to get some sleep. Hopefully I will sleep well and be able to get up feeling more refreshed than I did this morning!</u>

Thanks,

Alexia

Ray,

I had a productive day with homework and PLP things. <u>In addition, I slept in a bit extra this morning and am now wrapped up for the day. I'm going to lie down and hope to get to sleep a bit earlier than normal!</u>

Talk to you soon!

Alexia

Lesson: Get enough sleep.

Every successful person I have studied takes the time to make sure their physical, emotional, and spiritual health are taken care of. That doesn't mean they are perfect in these areas. They know they are not, and they work every day to get a little better. It is not about always being perfect and getting seven hours of sleep, it is about getting seven hours when you can, making an effort to keep yourself as a priority, and renewing your energy. There is a constant flow of new research on sleep and how getting enough improves your health, your cognitive skills, your willpower, and even helps you live longer. As a leader, be a good role model; eat right, exercise and plan to get seven hours of sleep each night and recommend your team members do the same.

Quick Tip: One of the keys to getting enough sleep is going to bed at a regularly scheduled time; and when you can't, planning ahead to make sure you get your full seven hours.

Opportunity: Think about what time you have to get up in the morning? Count backward eight hours and head to bed at that time. That gives you an hour to get settled and seven hours to sleep.

Lesson #35 - Spend Time with Energy Givers
Instead of Energy Suckers

Ray,

Today in PLP, it was a productive good day. At the hall, there is some extra drama that has slowly been draining me the last few weeks and today it kind of hit me. I talked to one of my friends outside of the situation and she was a huge help in getting past it and back to being productive!

I'm now ready for a good night's sleep!

Talk to you tomorrow!

Alexia

Lesson: Spend time with energy givers instead of energy suckers.

We all have "those" people in our lives. When you know you are going to have to spend time with them you feel your energy levels start to power down. All of your conversations with them are about drama and negativity. They spend hours telling you about how bad life is and how mistreated they are by everyone else in their lives. Limit the amount of time you spend with energy suckers. Unfortunately the energy suckers are often people we love and feel some sort off obligation toward. So we feel guilty for not hanging around and letting them power down our lives. You can still love them and appreciate them. You can spend time with them in short bursts, but be prepared to quickly disengage when you find your energy levels being drained.

Go find "energy givers" so you can grow and renew your energy levels. Find people who communicate rather than complain, and who listen and give rather than demand and take. Energy givers still have problems and they need someone to listen and empathize. The difference is they are not constantly telling hopeless and helpless stories. You can gain energy from listening to, empathizing with, and even helping some people. The difference in the energy suckers is they want you to wallow in their pain with them, not just lend a sympathetic ear. So be aware and spend less time with energy suckers and more with energy givers. Most importantly, make sure you are an energy giver as well.

Opportunity: Identify who the energy suckers are in your life and who the energy givers are.

Lesson #36 - Taking Care of Yourself Requires Intentional Effort

Ray,

I hope you had a safe flight! This weekend I have gotten a lot done for PLP, classes, and RA. <u>I have had to make a great effort to be sure and take some mental breaks so I didn't/ don't burn out!</u> I was also able to take some "me time", some exercising time, and some time to glance over my goals to help keep them in the forefront of my mind. I got a lot done but I still have A LOT to do tomorrow, so I am off to bed to try and get some sleep!

Talk to you soon,

Alexia

Lesson: Taking care of yourself requires intentional effort.

What many of us forget in setting our goals and priorities and dealing with the chaos of life, is that our health and happiness are the most important parts of the puzzle. If we don't take care of ourselves, we can't help others, we can't lead others, and we can't accomplish our goals. We have to take time to get plenty of rest, to exercise, to eat healthy, and to make sure we don't get mentally overwhelmed and burned out by the hundreds of options and obligations bombarding us on a daily basis. Make an intentional effort to set goals around taking care of yourself. Get plenty of sleep, exercise, and eat a healthy diet. Make sure your health and happiness are priorities that don't get lost in the chaos of life.

Opportunity: Set a goal related to taking care of yourself.

Nurture Relationships

Lesson #37 - Seize Opportunities to Make a Difference in Someone's Life

Alexia's Business Card

My story begins from the moment I was asked to join the Professional Leadership Program's Student Director Team. I was asked to join the team for the 2013-2014 academic year and gladly accepted the position, eager to help out those young and future professionals in the program. I was introduced to Alexia during one of my first meetings with the leadership group. I could immediately read the type of person that she was. She reflected a very positive light with her smile and her eager leadership style was to be admired. As I got to work with her and the team more and more, I quickly started to pick up on several other qualities that I found truly admirable in her. She was extremely prepared for every meeting, ready to discuss her plans and share her ideas with us. She had such a tenacious outlook on life, passing her courses with flying colors, despite her involvement with the Professional Leadership Program and her enrollment in honor classes. Her success was inspiring and from the moment I realized the type of person she was, I knew for a fact that she was destined for greatness in the future. She reminded the group that with a little bit of focus and determination, anything was possible and thanks to her leadership, we were able to have an extremely successful year with her.

After I met with Alexia to introduce myself and discuss my duties, she handed me her PLP business card. It contained her name, email address, phone number, and mini resume. I put it away inside my wallet. As the first half of the academic year went by, I started growing more and more respect and admiration towards Alexia. She was such a loving individual, ready to put others before herself. She didn't care if she lost sleep or even sacrificed her homework time, as long as she was able to help those in need of her help. She was such an inspirational figure, and at such a young age! Her attention to detail was very precise as well. I remember a specific day when instead of bringing in pizza or cake for our meeting, she brought in healthy sandwiches and salads. I then realized she did it with the intent to bring healthier food because she had heard me mention that I liked to eat healthy.

In November, around Thanksgiving time, I had plans to take a road trip to Kansas with my brother. My brother was going to record in a professional music studio located in Kansas, and I was accompanying him to record a few parts as well. We packed our musical instruments and several other items for the studio and started our drive from Denton. On our way there, as I was driving my brother's truck, I drove by an area on the freeway (around Oklahoma) that was full of black ice. I couldn't avoid the slippery spot and completely lost control of the truck. The black ice made the truck spin out of control and caused us to go from the right lane all the way to the left shoulder. There was no rail stopping us from falling into the deep ditch besides the freeway, so the black ice caused the truck to fly off of the freeway. While we were in the air, I quickly said a prayer, asking our heavenly father to protect us and declared that nothing would happen to either my brother or me. Once the truck hit the ditch, it continued to flip around for a couple of seconds until it stopped and landed on the right side of the truck. Soon after the truck landed, the engine caught on fire. My brother and I were trying to remain calm, knowing that we had to get out of the truck before it burst into flames. The only problem was that every door was caved in because of the impact, making it impossible for us to open any of them. We both tried punching the windows with no success, as we had landed in a very awkward spot that prevented us from using force on the windows effectively. Our time was running out as the engine fire started to spread around the front of the truck. Just when hope seemed to fade, my brother found an opening on the back of the truck where the narrow windows opened because of the impact. We both made it out of the truck from there; and shortly after, the entire truck caught on fire. Neither of us were able to salvage anything, not even our phones. The engine fire spread all over the truck, and the thick smoke that came out began to look like a thick grey cloud hovering over the truck. Despite the circumstances, we both managed to make it out of there alive and with very minor scratches, thanks to some help from above.

Once we both made it out, the police finally arrived, got our information, and dropped us off at a gas station in Oklahoma. They were unable to help us any further. After we made it to the gas station, I realized that I had no one to contact. Both of our phones were lost and I had no one's phone number memorized, except for my parents' phone numbers; but they live in California, many hours away. I gave them a phone call to explain the unfortunate event, and they felt terrible that they could not help us at that moment, given that it would take them hours to arrive. I then realized that I still had my wallet inside of my pocket. As I started looking inside it, I found only one item with a Denton phone number. It was Alexia's business card. I felt terrible for asking so much of her; but I gave her a call, knowing that she was our only hope of getting back to Denton. It was around 5:30 a.m., and I decided to give her a call. She answered immediately, with a very tired voice, asking who was calling. I told her it was me and explained our situation. She immediately got up, ready to do whatever she could. She was instantly ready to leave her house and help out. I told her that all I needed her to do was to go to my house in Denton, knock on the door until one of my roommates woke up, and explain the situation to them to see if they could help us out. I just needed to get in contact with one of my roommates, but Alexia was ready to pick me up! I didn't want to inconvenience her more than I already had, so we proceeded according to my plan and she drove to my house and started knocking. She must've been knocking for over five minutes. I told her that she had my permission to check to see if any of the doors were open, and she checked with hesitation but with no success. Finally, one of my roommates woke up and answered the door. She gave the phone to my roommate and I was able to explain our situation to him. We were finally able to formulate a plan for my roommate to pick us up from Oklahoma. We were finally coming back home and all thanks to Alexia. I just couldn't thank her enough.

The following days, my brother and I simply recovered and started replacing our losses as we could. We kept the incident private to prevent anyone from worrying. During our next PLP meeting, I thanked Alexia. I must've thanked her a dozen times and every time I did, I was the one who ended up being thanked for waking her up. She claimed that she already needed to wake up and start her day. That's just who she was. No one could inconvenience her. She was there to help others and truly exemplify what it means to be a "servant leader."

Alexia's tragic departure still barely makes any sense to me. I simply can't comprehend how someone with such a bright future was taken from us before her time, but I am sure that she is in a much better place, full of the same happiness and love that she reflected. Alexia did leave us with a recipe for success through her life though and I will always hold her dear memory close to me as motivation to exemplify what it means to be a true servant leader like her.

May Alexia rest in peace. She was a beautiful and genuine soul that will never be forgotten.   *Isaac Guajardo*

Lesson: Seize opportunities to make a difference in someone's life.

Leaders have busy lives with lots to do and many different obligations. There is a cacophony of demands pulling at your attention. It requires focus and discipline in setting your priorities to get the most important things done and not just the urgent. But by far the most important thing you can do is help a person in need. When someone is desperate for your help, that takes precedence over meetings, homework, tests, and anything else on your list. Put people first, especially your family. Seize opportunities to make a difference in the lives of others. You will be happier, more fulfilled, and more successful.

Opportunity: Think about who you can help today?

Lesson #38 - Leaders Fight for Their Team

Six Flags Student Director Trip

In October, the Student Directors of PLP planned a trip to Six Flags. We all felt it was important to build relationships outside of "work." We had purchased passes to go to the Fright Festival events; however, when we tried to enter they wouldn't let us in. There was some confusion about the wrong kind of tickets and needing extra tickets. Naturally none of us were okay with that response since broke college kids have little money and the tickets were $20 each. The security guard mentioned a customer service booth back at the main entrance. So we had to turn around and walk 20 minutes back to the front of the park and most of us assumed we would just leave then and go home. But as we got near the customer services booth, Alexia looked at me and said, "Oh no! We didn't pay $20 each to drive out here and leave." We began discussing how we were going to "nicely" persuade Six Flags to exchange our tickets for the ones we thought we had bought. I used my iPhone to do some research and could not find any fine print on the ticket or website suggesting that what they were saying was accurate. So we all waited in line with Alexia at the front. Alexia, wanting to be a lawyer, approached the "judge" of Six Flags and the court was in session. She was passionate for us, but gentle. She became very passionate in her defense because she cared about our not wasting our time and money. She wanted what was best for us.

Fortunately, her gentle approach and the lack of evidence from Six Flags to support their position, led to our all getting the correct tickets. Credit is also due to the very nice person working at Six Flags. The point is Alexia cared about us and was willing to fight for us. I tell this story to show that, even though we weren't best friends with her, friendship meant something to her. She fought for us with gentleness, despite her passion, showing that grace may abound in frustration.   *Austin Hatcher*

Lesson: Leaders fight for their team.

Leaders fight for their team and for what is right. Great opportunities to show your qualities as a leader arise when your team is not getting what they deserve or when you want to help get them something a little extra. Nothing brings a team together quicker than a common enemy or the feeling that being part of that team means something special. Step up when the time is right, and make sure your team gets what they deserve. Use your resources and energy to defend their honor or to make sure they are rewarded for their hard work and sacrifice.

Opportunity: Consider what battle you could fight to help your team get the recognition and success they deserve.

Lesson #39 - Include Your Team in the Solution

Ray,

Today I spoke with Rachel about the Student Director situation and although it is a curve ball, <u>I'm feeling pretty hopeful about the team finding a solution at our meeting tomorrow.</u> I have also completed all assignments for this week (except for two short quizzes that don't open until Friday at 12:01 AM) so I am feeling good about academics as well! I am done with my to do list and journaling and I am now off to bed!

Talk to you soon!

Alexia

Ray,

We had an interesting first meeting since the news of Student Director leaving. <u>I actually am VERY pleased with the team, their positivity, and the direction we are going from here.</u> I can't wait to fill you in fully next week!

As for my academic predicament, I have gotten a bit of the run around but now know which classes I have to choose from and who exactly to go to that has the final say if I can substitute or not. (Thankfully I also did extremely well when I took his class so hopefully he will remember me and know that I am a determined student who isn't trying to cut any corners). So I will be looking at the classes and setting up a time next week to actually meet with him. I also have two appointments set up in the next week with professors who can help guide me and give me knowledge that should help me in my goals to make a decision with CPA vs MBA.

Exercise, journals, and me time are still going well. I have also not felt hot or faint so hopefully my body is recovering well! Sorry for the extra-long email tonight!

Talk to you soon!

Alexia

Lesson: Include your team in the solution.

As a leader, even though you are taking full responsibility for the team, you don't have to solve every problem yourself. Reach out to the team for answers and for their expertise. Let them step up and create solutions to new challenges. They need the opportunity to lead as well and part of your job as a leader is to know when to be a follower. Reach out to your team for support. Let them solve most of the challenges. You will build a better team with many good leaders and a strong future.

Opportunity: Identify what problems you can let your team solve.

Lesson #40 - Servant Leadership is a Higher Purpose

Planning with Alexia and Seeing Her Heart:

Before the PLP program started Alexia and I were having great conversations about how we wanted to bring PLP to another level - how we wanted the next year to run smoother and add more value to the PLP members. She had a passion and a real heart that was clear to see. Alexia gave up her summer to just converse with the Directors and Student Directors, in order to help serve the people she had never met. Her passion was to serve others and this was not just a yearly goal or a "school" goal. No, it was so much more to her. Serving others for Alexia was a life style and her Higher Purpose. She was one of those rare people who cared about others more than herself. She would want this book to help you get to the next stage in your life. She didn't serve others for a block of time every week or just a few minutes a day, it was a way of life. It is very important to understand that it was woven into the fabric of Alexia. It was who she was at her core. This is not a fact that you learn, it is a commitment from the heart, a Higher Purpose. *Austin Hatcher*

Lesson: Servant leadership is a Higher Purpose.

Servant Leadership is <u>not</u> about you and what you can gain. It is about the people you lead and what you can do for them. Are you interested in a title for your resume, or do you believe in people and want to help them be happy and successful? Great leaders make sacrifices that could never be repaid by mere accolades. They make the sacrifices because they know they can matter and make a difference in the lives of the people on their teams. Don't lead for you, lead for them. Your contribution will be immeasurable and you will live a life of fulfillment.

Opportunity: Consider your motivation; are you leading for you or for others?

Lesson #41 - Take Opportunities to Spend Time with Team Members

Ray,

Today I finished moving everything into the resident's hall so I got plenty of exercise moving and lifting for so many hours. I also picked up a friend from the airport, which is why I'm a bit later with my update than normal. But I have done my journals and am off to bed! See you in the morning!

Alexia

Lesson: Take opportunities to spend time with team members.

As a leader, your role is to help the team reach its goals and become successful. That means helping out the individuals on the team, so they can become successful members of the team. Spending time individually with your team members will help you understand their needs and motivations. It will give you information that will help you know who would be best for what activity because of their personal goals, interests, or experience. When you have the opportunity to have lunch with, provide a lift for, or otherwise help out a team member, take advantage of it. It will help make the team better and make you a better leader.

Opportunity: Identify one thing you can do today to help a team member.

Lesson #42 - Leaders Care for Others

My name is Eric Johnson and I was Alexia's Hall Director for the majority of her time at Honors Hall. I have been working within residence life for going on seven years now, and I can honestly say that Alexia was one of the most driven people I have ever met. But behind that drive was someone that truly cared for other people and her family. Her residents knew her as someone they truly could come and talk to regardless of the issue. It could have been a leaky faucet or some sort of crisis and Alexia wouldn't miss a beat. The way she consistently talked about her family made me as her supervisor want to grow and connect with mine in a deeper way. She truly was a one-of-a-kind young lady and someone that I will truly miss seeing around my hall and the UNT Campus.

You were one of the greatest people I knew. You never said no to anyone and always helped in any way.   *Ratinder Sandhu*

One of the world's up and coming leaders…Alexia Ardeleanu, such a strong woman in leadership. I served as a Student Director for the PLP program with her as our President. She spent much more time than most of us have developing new leaders.   *Karolyn Hernandez*

Alexia and Humility: I only ever remember Alexia listening first and then responding. She was always willing to hear others first. Alexia never assumed that she knew best, but rather invited feedback and new ideas. She was coachable and wanted to learn. The qualities just listed are those of anyone great. Champions have a great ability, but still keep themselves grounded. Alexia chose to validate others first by hearing them rather than just speaking her wisdom.   *Austin Hatcher*

I lived in Honors Hall my freshman year and saw Alexia all the time. She always had a smile on her face and always took time to make sure all of her residents were doing alright adjusting to college. On the night of my last final of the Fall semester in 2012, I was up late cramming for a Geology final that I had to get an A on to maintain a B in the class. I was absolutely unprepared and Alexia sat down with me, without being asked and studied for two hours so I could be better prepared. I ended up getting a 96 on that final, thanks to her. Alexia impacted the lives of so many students at UNT. *– Jessse Brackeen.*

From Alexia's Journal: *I dream of the day when I am stable in my career, have a husband & two kids, and can help support my parents who have no time off to really relax & enjoy life. I hope to keep them from having to work until they reach their time to go.*

Lesson: Leaders care for others.

"People don't care how much you know until they know how much you care"   Theodore Roosevelt

Leaders reach out to others on a regular basis. They adopt an attitude of "How can I help?" rather than "What can I get?" They listen and place priority on the needs of the team. They are able to show they care by the focus and attention they give to the needs of others. The more you help others, the more happiness and fulfillment you will find in your own life and the more opportunities you will have to lead.

Opportunity: Ask yourself who needs to know you care.

Alexia Being Recognized for Her Leadership

Lesson #43 - Seize Opportunities to Teach Others

Ray,

Not to much more has happened since I last emailed you. I did put on an RA program focused on professional development, and I had a pretty good turnout! People were very thankful for my putting it on and it was nice to see I made a difference! Otherwise, I worked desk and studied a bit more and am now off to journal and go to bed! Talk to you soon!

Alexia

Ray,

To keep it interesting for the residents, I set up jeopardy with different categories like resumes, interviewing, career fair, etc. Every time they answered a question, I gave some background as to why that was the correct answer and some more information on the topic. At the end, I let them ask any questions they still had and had handouts with all the career fair dates and professional workshops dates, as well as booklets of information on building your résumé and preparing for an interview.

Alexia

Lesson: Seize opportunities to teach others.

If you want to be seen as a leader, find ways to help others learn more. You will improve your skills and become better at any topic you teach and you will help other team members improve their skills as well. Also look for opportunities to learn from others and encourage them to teach the skills they excel at.

Opportunity: Identify what you are really good at that you could teach to someone else. Think about what skill you would like to learn, and consider whether committing to teach a class would provide you the motivation to learn that new skill.

Lesson #44 - You Can Be a Friend and a Leader

Alexia had the best blend of fun and work. Anytime it was late and I was tucked away in my stairwell getting my work done, I would look forward to seeing her on rounds because she was a fantastic one for banter. At the same time, when she laid down a rule or reminded me of one, she meant it. It wasn't ever overtly harsh, just firm, and she managed to still be the person I bantered with. It isn't easy to carry yourself that way; she rocked it, and I really admired it. She was always ready to smile and laugh with me, and that helped me feel more at home in Honors than I would have otherwise.

Her work ethic was incredible; a few times I tried to get her into tea because she was sick and at the desk - not even because she was working, but just because she felt the need to study. She took incredible notes; they were full blown color-coordinated notes, and she didn't mind my curious questions and examinations thereof. When she worked, she really worked. Dedication is a virtue, and she had it in spades. I could never convince her to really like tea but she was always game to try my new blends.

I would never say her last name right, on purpose, because it was so much ridiculous fun for me to find new convoluted ways to say it. It was a little game we had, trying to one-up each other with jokes or jibes, and it never felt mean. Her badinage was one of my favorite things about Honors. *Jena*

Alexia was a true, kind, and beautiful friend. She was an inspiration for me daily and watching the way she approached life taught me how to believe in myself when it seemed impossible for me to do so. In some of my darkest hours she could pull me through by just being there. I feel truly blessed knowing my sweet friend, for all of our wonderful memories and for her sharing her heart with me. *Ashley Dixon*

This year for Christmas, Alexia gathered the five of us girls together; her, Caitlin, Shannon, Kristen, and I, to give us all our Christmas presents. She told us how important we were to her, and that this was our last semester being RA's and all living on campus together. She, Shannon, and Kristen would be in apartments, Caitlin would be graduated, and I'd hopefully be at Disney (I didn't know if I'd get it at the time, but she always had faith in me.) She gave us all matching bracelets that say, "love much...laugh often...LIVE WELL"; so we'd always remember our friendship and being together. Alexia was selfless and always put others first. I am only one of hundreds of people who had their lives touched by Alexia. She always went out of her way to help others.   *Suzanne Peterson*

Lesson: You can be a friend and a leader.

Leadership is not about separating yourself from others; it is about becoming an integral part of the team. The more friendships you have on the team, the better your chance of influencing its direction. Your friends become a coalition of leaders who share common goals and values. They can lead when their strengths are needed and you can lead when your strengths are more helpful. You will trust your friends and they will trust you which will help move initiatives forward, even when the outcome is uncertain. Your friends will be more honest with you about what the team needs and how you can become a better leader.

Also, people want to know their leaders care about them. They want to follow leaders they like and admire. Be the best person you can be, so you will stand out and earn the right to lead, but don't forget that includes being a real friend to others and helping them grow and improve as well. You will be happier and more fulfilled as a leader if you nurture your friendships and make them a key part of the team's success.

Opportunity: Identify those on your team who need a friend.

At Yogurt Story Spring 2012 - another time that Alexia had to bribe me with sweets before I would start my homework. Alexia set such high standards for herself, and just by being in her life, you started to raise yours without realizing yet. Alexia brought out the best in people. Suzanne

Bessie, Alexia, and Constantin Ardeleanu – Prom Night

Lesson #45 - Offer Your Gift of Leadership to Those

Who Might Get Left Behind

Ray,

Today has been quite a day! I woke up this morning with a horrible headache so I went back to sleep for a bit. I then got up and got some more of my project done before heading off to class. I then had SD office hours where I went over my SD Scorecard with Rachel and had a very productive conversation! I also spoke with Tina some more. She should have reached out to you tonight. She was hoping to sit in with our meeting tomorrow after PLP but I told her to email you and get your okay as well. That way, like you said, it really is her making the first step. After office hours, I went with a friend and got a massage, which was very helpful in alleviating my headache! I then came home, worked the front desk, did a little work out, showered, and am now off to bed feeling great about an all around productive day!

Can't wait to meet with you tomorrow!

Alexia

Lesson: Offer your gift of leadership to those who might get left behind.

Alexia made sure everyone was taken care of. One of the girls in her group, Tina (I changed the name to protect her privacy), was struggling with time management, participation, and concern about what happens after college. She was overwhelmed by school and all her activities. Alexia took special time to work with her on her goals, and assembled a team of mentors and friends to consult with her, and then Alexia coached her on a daily and weekly basis. She kept the team informed of Tina's progress and made herself available until Tina was able to successfully graduate.

As a leader you won't have time to take care of everyone and various followers will drop out of the team for their own personal reasons; but it is worthwhile to evaluate whether someone can be helped, and with a few nudges from you, get back on track. Reach out for help from others and don't try to do it all alone. Offer to help the person in need, but don't try to force them to do anything or even expect they will respond. Your leadership is a gift. They may or may not decide to accept your gift. They may not want to take advantage of the opportunities you provide them. But offer your gift of leadership any-way. Helping one person get back on track will make it all worthwhile.

Opportunity: Think about who needs a little nudge and a little help from you to be successful.

Lesson #46 - Take Time for Appreciation and Recognition

Ray

Tonight I wrote a bunch of thank you cards for all the leaders and execs at McKesson that helped make the internship so memorable for me. I did a 30 minute work-out. I am writing my journal and am off to bed!

Alexia

Karolyn,

Great update for everyone! Thank you so much for this! Melissa has completed the hours and was having lunch with the director who can verify that last Friday so she should just need to turn in the form. I will double check though!

Alexia

Lesson: Take time for appreciation and recognition.

We are often busy with the chaos of life and forget to take time to show people how much we appreciate their help and support. But it is important to take that time, not just for them but for ourselves. It makes us feel better to reflect on things we are grateful for and to share those feelings with other people. Successful leaders make time to show appreciation and recognition for the people who make a difference and who make things happen.

Opportunity: Think about how you can recognize and appreciate someone today.

Lesson #47 - Create Time for Team Bonding

Ray,

Tonight I had a lot of me time and friends time. The staff all just finished watching some movies and I am now done with my journals and off to bed!

Alexia

Ray,

Today was a productive day full of staff bonding, training, meeting with Rachel to catch up on PLP things and some McKesson work tonight. I'm now doing journals and am off to bed!

Alexia

Ray,

Today I had a pretty easy day at work and then *we had a social outing for the PLP SD's! A bunch of us went to Fright Fest and had a lot of fun hanging out,* outside of the office!

I just got home and am off to bed! We have a big PLP volunteer event in the morning! Have a wonderful weekend!

Alexia

Ray,

Today at work, I had a mid-year review with my manager and discussed what the next year or two looks like concerning my balancing classes and McKesson. The discussion went really well and it looks like the plan I have had in mind will be feasible on their side as well!

Staff meeting tonight went great as well! _I suggested that next week's meeting be a more casual meeting with dinner and a movie afterward._ Everyone agreed so hopefully that will be a good first step to getting back to being more of a cohesive team again! I had some me time today and otherwise have been studying like crazy! I'm now off to get some sleep! Talk to you tomorrow!

Alexia

Ray,

Hope you had a wonderful weekend and a happy Monday! My day has mainly been McKesson work and meetings, _but we did have some staff bonding tonight!_ After our RA meeting, we all went down to the common room and put on a movie and all hung out! Steve, our boss, decided to watch football instead, but the rest of us had a great time! Shannon and Caitlin were even talking and laughing together so that's a great start!

It's been a pretty great day! I finished closing down the front desk and doing all my RA on call duties, I am in a great mood, and I am now off to try and get some rest! Talk to you soon!

Alexia

Ray,

Today was a long day working on RA things. After dinner I had a slight headache so I took a long refreshing nap! _We then, as a staff, took a trip to get frozen yogurt and had a movie night!_ I am now finishing my journals and heading to bed! Talk to you soon!

Alexia

Lesson: Create time for team bonding.

As leaders we often get caught up in the business of our teams and forget that teams are really about people and personal interactions. The leader and everyone else on the team feel so busy that getting together outside of the regularly scheduled meetings can seem like an extra burden. But team bonding yields significant rewards that can eventually save everyone time and bring a higher level of commitment to the team. Spending time together casually, helps team members become aware of how much they have in common so they are more open to the diversity of thought and opinions brought to the team meetings. Bonding events help forge informal alliances that enable teams to get things done quicker and more efficiently. Casual bonding experiences also create friendships that result in more loyalty and commitment to the team overall. Create time for bonding events and other opportunities for your team to gather informally. Create formal bonding events as well as ad-hoc social activities. Find time for a quick meal or movie with a few team members. Your team will be happier, more efficient, and more successful.

Opportunity: Schedule and organize two team bonding activities even if you're not the official leader of the group.

Lesson #48 – Find Someone You Can Talk To

Ray,

Sorry you haven't heard much from me this week... My schedule has been totally messed up from usual!

Good news is that I had for sure received three As and it's looking likely for the other two classes to be As as well!

I have been taking plenty of me time and exercise time in between all the craziness that has been this past week!

There have been some roller coasters around here with things seeming fine and then little things happen and they blow up into much bigger than necessary. However <u>Suzanne has been great for me to vent to for a minute or two and then help me forget about it and not worry! In addition, I spent some time catching up with Kristen, one of our other friends who has also been put in the middle of the RA drama and that REALLY helped. Although the issues around the hall haven't gone away, I feel like I at least have more of a happy and positive support system than I felt like I did a few weeks ago, especially through Suzanne and Kristen concerning a lot of the extra stress related to the hall and the other girls.</u>

I think all of us girls having some time away from each other during break may help A LOT too!

(Sorry it's a longer email, but I just wanted to give you an update on it all!)

Talk to you soon!

Alexia

Lesson: Find someone you can talk to.

We all need good friendships in our lives, but as a leader it is especially important. You need someone you can trust, bounce ideas off of, and safely vent to from time to time. You need people who understand and support your level of responsibility as well as your personal frustrations. You need friends who can help you stay grounded and remember that besides being a leader, you are also a human being with all the frustrations, emotions, and challenges of everyone else on the team. Seek out and nurture positive friendships. Make time for people who support you as a leader, but also care about you as a friend. Make time to be a good friend to them as well.

Opportunity: Make a list of friends you can talk to.

Lesson #49 - Ask for Help

Ray,

Sorry for no email last night. By the time I was done with on call stuff, I passed out!

Monday while at work, <u>I talked to my boss about being overwhelmed with everything going on, and he was very helpful</u>. He said that school comes first and if I ever need to take a half day or day off, not to feel bad about it.

Yesterday, with classes being cancelled, I took some time to sleep in and decompress in the morning. Then I went straight to studying and was productive most of the day, taking breaks to keep myself from wearing out.

Today, the world has cut me some slack! <u>I talked with Rachel and she told me to miss after hours next week and the career fair the following week. She also suggested that during the last hour of presentation each week I step out and study since they are all topics I have heard before.</u> In addition, I found out one of my exams that was scheduled for tomorrow is getting pushed back to Tuesday since we didn't have class yesterday. That takes a little more pressure off of tomorrow!

On a side note, scorecards are due next Wednesday so I will take some time this weekend to get mine up to date and email it to you to see what changes you would make to it.

Thanks and talk to you soon!

Alexia

Ray,

Today, in addition to all my other daily activities and schedule, <u>I met with Professor Ellis and got her perspective on my future career path.</u> We will have a lot to talk about come Monday! Hope you have a great Friday!

Alexia

Ray,

Today I talked to Rachel and the remaining SDs about the new SD situation. It looks like we are headed toward bringing them on board fully!

Also, today was the career fair. We got an early start on recruiting and even gained some new possible mentors/sponsors for the program!

I just finished an assignment due tomorrow at noon and, ironically, when I opened my email, I saw my professor emailed me that there have been some issues accessing the online assignment and we now have 24 extra hours to complete it... I may have stayed up longer than planned to complete it but at least I am ahead now!

Overall it's been a good day!

Have a wonderful night and I will talk to you tomorrow!

Alexia

Ray,

This morning I slept in a bit, did a little workout, and then headed off to class. During office hours for PLP, Rachel, Billy, and I had a good conversation about some issues that need to be discussed with the Student Directors. We will be having that conversation tomorrow so hopefully we will see some improvements moving forward! Otherwise, I have just done some homework and worked desk this evening. I'm now off to bed!

Talk to you soon!

Alexia

Ray,

Since I saw you last today, I had a great meeting with Roy and learned a lot about the structure of the GMAT and how to go about tackling it, and I also got some advice for looking at which schools to consider. It was extremely productive!

I got home just in time for the GA at the hall and then had some friends time with Suzanne watching one of our favorite tv shows to watch together. We haven't had much time for the two of us this week so we got to hangout a bit and catch up! It was a great way to end the night!

Thank you so much for everything you have done to help me out both personally and professionally. I can't imagine this semester without you as my mentor!

Talk to you soon!

Alexia

Lesson: Ask for help.

Unfortunately, as much as we would like to, we can't do everything ourselves. We need others to listen, give advice, and help. As a leader we are tasked with using all of our resources to accomplish the team goals, and that especially means reaching out to the people around us. You will be more successful as a leader if you can get outside input and advice. Seek out other leaders, mentors, and experts in various fields. Keep an active list of people you can call and turn to when you are facing difficult challenges. Match their expertise to the challenge. Find out what they know about the situation or how they have handled similar situations. Listen to their advice. What kind of perspectives can they offer that differ from yours? The wider your group of advisors, the more success you will have. Seek out mentors and advisors. Share your challenges and ask for their advice. They will usually be pleased to help.

Opportunity: Make a list of friends and advisors you can reach out to for help and wisdom.

Lesson #50 - Create Time for Family and Friends, Even in the Middle of Chaos

Ray,

So today I got a lot of little things done for my classes. It was A LOT of reading! I also had some time to get some little household type chores done, take some me time, and get some exercising in.

This evening for me was overtaken by RA things. I spent two hours working through a harassment situation for one of the residents and finished that up just in time to run to get ready for our fire drill. Those events pushed back my plans to go see a movie with friends. Although later than planned, we did still go which was a nice change of pace after the heavy topics that filled this evening! I'm now exhausted and heading off to bed! Talk to you soon!

Alexia

Ray,

Today I drove home to Houston, spent some time with friends, and now am writing in my journals and headed to bed!

Alexia

Ray,

Today mom and I had a relaxing girls day bumming around town. I also ran around playing with my dog for quite a while today for some exercise! I have written in my journals and mom and I are now watching a movie while we lay in bed to fall asleep.

Alexia

Ray,

Today I relaxed and spent more time with my mom and got some exercise in, and I am now getting ready to do my journals and head to bed!

Alexia

Ray,

Today was, over all, a pretty good day! _I played volleyball intramurals tonight and it was so much fun! I just finished a quiz and packing for this weekend's trip!_ I can't wait to catch you up on all of the PLP recent events as well as RA! See you Monday!

Alexia

Hi Ray!

This long weekend was much needed! I spent some time with family/friends, catching up on my rest, and being productive. It was a good mix and I feel a lot better going into this week!

Thanks and talk to you soon!

Alexia

Ray,

I had some fun play time after a department meeting with McKesson and _I had some great friends time tonight to help vent a bit and help mentally relieve some stress which was awesome!_ I did my journals and am now headed to bed! Talk to you soon,

Alexia

Lesson: Create time for family and friends, even in the middle of chaos.

Make time for family and friends. Don't let the chaos of life derail those plans. The people in your best relationships are understanding and supportive, and therefore easier to blow off. But those relationships are also the most important things in your life and a key to your success and happiness. Every now and then, the chaos of life will interfere with your time with those important people. But don't let it postpone those visits indefinitely. Make sure they happen on a regular basis and you get your needed energy boost and support from your best relationships. More importantly, you need your opportunity to give back to those relationships, as it will make both you and the relationship stronger. As a leader you need confidence, energy, and diverse opinions you can count on. Those all come from your positive relationships. Make time to nurture your important relationships, especially in the middle of chaos.

Opportunity: Make a list of your most important relationships. Reach out and schedule time with them today.

Our goal for this book was that you would learn leadership through Alexia's real life experiences, examples, and challenges. We hoped to preserve her memory and embody her wonderful example to live on. Alexia was a leader, a teacher, a student, a friend, and most importantly, a wonderful sister and daughter. She made the most out of her life and we hope you have found a few lessons that will help you do the same.

You can donate to the Alexia Ardeleanu Memorial Fund at: **https://one.unt.edu/alexia**

Don't Cry For Alexia by Ray White

Don't cry for Alexia, she is in a far better place now. Cry for our loss of a wonderful young lady who had a talent for positively impacting the lives of others. Cry for our pain and deep sense of grief that threatens to overwhelm us and seems like it will be with us forever.

But don't cry for Alexia. Instead, let's honor her memory. Let's make others' lives better just as she has made ours better.

Alexia loved and respected her parents. She never showed entitlement or animosity like so many young people in all generations have done. When her dad was in the hospital for surgery, she worried about him and made time to be home and help him recover. She never spoke of it as a burden or duty, but as an opportunity to help someone she loved and respected. She was so excited about her mother's new job, because she knew how much less stress the better hours and weekends off would provide for her mom. She appreciated all the time and investment her parents made in helping her get her education and succeed in life.

Don't cry for Alexia; honor her memory by loving and respecting your parents.

Alexia was proud of her brother. She told me "He is different than me, but he has found his path and I am so happy for him." She talked about and embraced his diversity rather than judging his differences.

Don't cry for Alexia; honor her by embracing the diversity of all our brothers and sisters. Support them and help them succeed at being them rather than asking them to be like us.

Alexia pursued excellence for noble reasons. Alexia studied hard and took classes to get great scores on her GMAT and LSAT, even while she was taking a full course load and working two jobs. I quizzed her about her motivation to work so hard - asking about the usual assumptions of getting good scores, to get into a good college, to get a great job, so eventually she could be rich and successful. But that was not her plan at all. She wanted high scores so she could get scholarships, so her parents would not have the extra burden of paying for her graduate school. Her Plan B was to take a few years off and work to save money to pay for her extra schooling. Alexia owned her excellent outcomes. She made them happen and greatly appreciated rather than expected the help she got along the way.

Don't cry for Alexia; honor her by creating excellence in your life and not placing the burden on others.

Alexia made her work more than a job. Alexia didn't want to just have a job as a Resident's Assistant. We talked several times about how she wanted to work with her RA team to become the best dorm on campus. She wanted to impact the residents' lives and provide a wonderful experience. Alexia didn't just do a job; she brought her heart and passion to her work to create a fulfilling experience.

Don't cry for Alexia; honor her by creating purpose in your work and finding fulfillment in how you can help others.

Alexia implemented change. I work with many students and offer tips to help them be happier and more successful. I consider it a win if 2 of the 10 tips I offer are implemented. Small changes can make a big difference in people's lives. Alexia implemented every tip I ever offered. She implemented them with excitement and vigor and shared them with her friends. She constantly worked to improve her life and make it better. Then she reached out and helped others improve their lives.

Don't cry for Alexia; honor her by making changes to make your life better, and along the way help someone else make their life better.

I don't cry for Alexia. I know she is in a better place. I cry for my loss and my pain and my deep sadness. But I know that soon I will get past this grief and work to honor Alexia. I will learn from her example and try to be half the person she has taught us to be. Alexia led by example. She loved and respected her parents, embraced the diversity of her brothers and sisters, pursued excellence for noble reasons, turned a job into a fulfilling part of her life, and implemented changes to continuously make her life and the lives of others better.

Don't cry for Alexia; honor her memory.

You can donate to the Alexia Ardeleanu Memorial Fund at: **https://one.unt.edu/alexia**

Memories to Honor Alexia

"Over the years I have come to understand that God works in mysterious ways, but I cannot wrap my head around this one. Rest in peace Alexia Ardeleanu, you are in a better place now, but will forever be missed." *–Sujey Franco*

"A beautiful soul that will never be forgotten. May she rest in peace" *– Isaac Guajardo*

"I've spent the last year serving PLP with this amazing individual and still can't believe she's now gone. She was such an amazing person and it wasn't her time. I know she's in heaven right now but she will truly be missed here on earth." *–Angelique Davis*

"Dear Alexia, I feel your absence and this hurts me so much. I wish you were here with us, and I would be behind you again as one of my favorite women leaders! I had no doubt for your success and inspiring other women as a leader. Now, I feel lonely and sad that we need to build new women leaders without you. I wish you were here with us, I miss you my sweet leader. Rest in peace, we will continue to raise new female leaders by remembering you." *–Eva Gulin*

"One of the world's up and coming leaders, dear to my heart passed away... My heart is broken for the loss of Alexia Ardeleanu, such a strong woman in leadership. I served as a Student Director for the PLP program with her as our President. Sad to know that someone who spent much more time than most of us have trying to develop new leaders, and had such a strong future going for her, has lost her life this soon. Prayers go out to her friends and family. Still hard to believe. She will always be remembered....God please take good care of her." *–Karolyn Hernandez*

"Alexia Ardeleanu, your leadership as president in PLP was remarkable and I am truly blessed to have been your pledge brother and friend. I was looking forward to watching you kick [butt] as a lawyer, but I know God has greater plans for you. Rest in peace Alexia, you will be missed." *–Nehlin Mehra*

"With a heavy heart I can truly say that Alexia was great person. Always pushing us from our comfort zone to help us grow as professionals and as individuals. You were a great President and an awesome leader to our cluster. You will be dearly missed." *–Melissa Argueta*

"I would like to send my condolences to the Ardeleanu family and the rest of the PLP family in this time of bereavement. Alexia was an absolute joy to be around - and exemplified servant leadership in every way." *–Christopher Jackson*

"You were the true definition of a servant leader Alexia Ardeleanu I will be praying for your family." *-Alexis Harrison*

"Blessed and thankful to have known such a sweet, genuine, and kind person and amazing leader who will remain an inspiration and role model for us all. Rest in peace Alexia Ardeleanu." *–Anisha Upponi*

"I know a lot of us are dealing with the grief of losing a loved one right now. My heart goes out to the many impacted by the loss. We all took part in the joy of knowing one of the best leaders at the college of business at UNT and one of the nicest girls in Kingwood High School. She was an inspiration to others and had such a bright future. We will never understand why the good die young. Rest in peace sweet angel, and may you rest in the Lord's kingdom and always remind us to hold true to business ethics in the way you would have. Thank you for all of your help in developing talent in PLP, and all of the smiles you shared with us." *–Vanessa Arias*

"Your smile and kind words I will treasure. You were taken too soon and yet you made a huge impact on so many lives; you were a true leader. My condolences to the family and the UNT/PLP community." *–Regina Torres*

"My heart is breaking for her family. Please lift them up in prayer and our whole UNT/ PLP family as we remember her legacy of love for others, encouraging attitude, driven personality, and constant smile." *–Rachel Cleveland*

"My heart is so heavy right now. Alexia Ardeleanu was a friend of mine and a fellow PLP Alum and Student Director. She was such a go-getter and had a true servant leader's heart. It is proven over and over again, how short life is. Please, please remember her family in your prayers as will I." *–Destiny Johnson*

"She was our up-and-coming leader that I will never forget! Hard to believe she's gone. In my prayers." *–Rudy Cerda*

"You were one of the greatest people that I knew. You never said no to anything and always helped in any way. I know that you are in a better place and my prayers go out to you and your family." *–Ratinder Sandhu*

"Heaven gained an angel today. Alexia, I wouldn't be the person I am today if it weren't for your drive and inspiration. You will be greatly missed by all and never forgotten." *–Laura Poole*

"She was such a good friend and always a great motivator for those around her. She always had a high standard for herself and surpassed it with her unmatched drive. As sad and heart-broken as I am, I'm so happy to know she is in a much better place and I'll be seeing her again one day." *–Jamie Graham*

"She was a great person. I know she would have done so many great things." –*Blake Jackson*

"Alexia was one of the most beautiful, intelligent, mature & wise young ladies I'd ever met. She had such a positive impact on Lisa over the years. She taught Lisa how to be assertive and be a go-getter. We will never forget that. May she rest in peace in the arms of our Lord. God bless your family." - *Teresa and Tony Piraino*

"My heart goes out to her family. The world lost an amazing young lady. RIP. She'll be missed, dearly." –*Mardon Navalta*

"Our collective hearts go out to Alexia's family. She was a beam of light that illuminated all of those she encountered." –*Claire Billingsley*

"Rest in peace Alexia Ardeleanu. She was such a magnificent individual and did an amazing job as President of the Professional Leadership Program last year. She was such an amazing person and had an infectious personality. I will never forget that beautiful smile and the light of energy she had. I'm truly heartbroken. Alexia, you are in God's hands now and definitely made a difference in my life and everyone who knew you. Rest easy, beautiful angel, rest easy." -*Jordyn Williams*

"It's hard to put into words how I feel when a dear friend is lost after so many others have said the same things I want to say, but that's just it. All of those condolences and messages of love and caring define what you mean to us and define you as a person. Alexia Ardeleanu, so many people cared for you and I'm saddened to see you go, but I promise I'll learn some sort of two-steppin' country song at Billy Bob's, and when I get to the Pearly Gates we'll reunite and dance to Marshall Tucker or something." -*Trey Yates*

"Stephen and I watched as Alexia grew into a beautiful young woman from the most adorable and loveable young girl. She was lovely on the outside, but even more beautiful on the inside, a truly exceptional person. We will never forget her genuine smile that would brighten up a cloudy day or her pleasant attitude and how she would approach everyone, both the very young and the elderly. All the children would run to greet her the minute they saw her in church. Most of all, we will never forget her angelic voice as she sang in the choir." *-Lana and Stephen*

"Alexia's bright mind and beautiful spirit were gifts that I will treasure forever. It was truly a privilege to know her, work with her, and to witness the goodness she brought to the world." *-Jeff Clayton*

"I know and believe that everything happens for a reason but this is really hard to understand. Rest in perfect peace Alexia" *-Anushka Maya Singh*

"We have never forgotten Alexia's kindness and welcoming feeling that was shown to us the very first day we walked in St. Cyril. Alexia was one of the first people I talked to that day. I was in awe of her maturity and kindness. I think she must have been 13 or 14 years old. She had the big smile and even though she didn't know us (me and my kids) she went out of of her way to make us feel welcome. She was just a kid herself but she was mature beyond her years. In 2007 we had a house fire and I will never ever forget how Alexia handed me an envelope with cash in it the next time I was in church. She had asked for donations for us, from kids at her school. We received help from many people at that time but her thoughtfulness was beyond anything I ever expected. She was truly the kind of person that made you feel better just for having met her. Just a beautiful person, inside and out. I am so sorry for your loss." *-Larissa McLain*

"When I first met Alexia, I thought she was older because off her maturity and intelligence. Since then, I have looked up to her as if she were older. As many people have shared with you, Alexia was an inspiration to us all. It is evident she made a lasting and positive difference in this world. She touched the lives of many and had such grace. Her natural ability to lead blew us all away. I loved singing with her in the choir and hearing her beautiful voice. I remember the only reason I started making my dad a full plate of food for coffee hour was because I saw how kind Alexia was to make you a plate. It was the sweetest thing to see how she had such a heart for others and put their needs before her own. Alexia has always been an angel and her love will always be remembered. She was a perfect example of God's love. May her memory be eternal!" *-Kaitlin Nickolas*

"Alexia was one of the sweetest people I've had the pleasure to know and work with. Accomplished beyond her years is definitely to say the least. She was extraordinary. I admired her work and her intelligence, but most of all, her kindness. Alexia was brilliant and shared it with others. Her smile, laugh, and friendship will be missed." *-Lorena Ortiz*

"I grieve for you for the loss of your beautiful talented daughter, Alexia. We have over 5400 students in the college of business, but few make such a deep and lasting impression as Alexia did. She had a hug for everyone, no matter who they were. She was an inclusive leader who made everyone feel valued. Here intellectual gifts shone in and beyond the classroom. She was not just our student, she was my friend and I will miss her dearly. My thoughts and prayers are with you." *-Marilyn Wiley – Senior Associate Dean – University of North Texas*

"Alexia was a source of calm for Suzanne and showed her the benefits of planning ahead. Alexia was goal oriented and thoughtful and again Suzanne benefited from having a friend demonstrate those attributes. Alexia was also a great leader. I'm not sure Suzanne would say it this way, but I think Alexia modelled for her the young woman Suzanne would like to become. Alexia impacted our family and we will never forget her." *–Kim Peterson*

"I was privileged to get to know Alexia when my daughter Ashley Quinn had her car accident and Alexia would come to the hospital time and time again. She would walk in with a smile on her face and brought such cheer into a dreary room. She spent a lot of time with me during Ashley's recovery. She laughed with me, she cried with me, and she offered encouragement. It seems like she was always there when it was time to move rooms (and we moved a lot) and she would take charge and start grabbing things and loading up. I never had to ask her for her help. She was there when Ashley started to talk and when we were able to get Ashley to throw a ball and hit things on a shelf and it all fell off. We laughed and laughed. She was there after Ashley came home from the hospital and continued to show her love and support. I am so blessed to have the memories of her in my heart. Alexia, you were such a genuine and loving person. You will be missed but never forgotten by all the people you have touched in such a short time. Rest in Peace sweet girl, you are loved!"   *-Melony Quinn*

"Love you Alexia. You can boss me around in heaven. We will miss you sooo much, but never forget you." *–Austin Hatcher*

"I am very blessed and lucky to have had the chance to work with Alexia. She was the brightest and most helpful person that I have ever met. She will never be forgotten and will always be in our heart."   *-Kevin Theang*

"Alexia was an especially cherished member for the UNT family and we were honored she chose UNT to pursue a degree in finance and accounting. It's clear that she was driven and passionate about her education, excelling as a student and a a leader. She was the best kind of role model – one who gave as much as she received. She will be remembered fondly by her fellow students, her Honors College family, her Professional Leadership Program family, her professors and her entire UNT family. Her legacy will live on through the many lives she touched through her leadership and positive, generous spirit."   *-Neal Smatresk – President University of North Texas*

"It's hard to find the words to express my deep sorrow and sympathy over the loss of Alexia. However, it's very easy to share my thoughts in celebration of her life. The times when she & Kaitlin would stop by our home for some home-cooking and respite from the Honors Hall were always wonderful, especially the way they always started and ended with Alexia's twinkling eyes, big smile, and warm hugs. But I really got to know her when she stayed with us last December to finish the week at McKesson before the holidays. Each evening upon returning from work, she'd change into comfy clothes then join us at the dinner table, where she'd tell us all about her day, plans, and stories about you & Apollo. Later she'd curl up in a chair next to my gift-wrapping table and keep me company, while I wrapped. As she shared of herself, I was struck by how Alexia just bubbled over with love for you, her friends, and her life. Though she worked hard toward her goals for the future...she was also exceedingly present, as though squeezing the most from every moment. I will always treasure your precious daughter. Memory Eternal!"   *-Valerie Kite*

"My Dearest Alexia - You are so very kind...You make it very easy to be a parent. You are always ready to do for others, just like your mother. I am thankful for your love and your kind hearted loving comments. You, my dear child, never cease to amaze me in your maturity, your gracious heart, and loving soul. You are one of God's greatest gifts to mom and me!!! Stay strong in soul and in faith! May God continue to keep you in His care! Love you more than I can ever express in words or deeds! Love ya Scump!!!!" *-Constantin Ardeleanu – written prior to Alexia's passing*

You can donate to the Alexia Ardeleanu Memorial Fund at:

https://one.unt.edu/alexia

Made in the USA
San Bernardino, CA
02 May 2017